VISUAL RESEARCH

VISUAL RESEARCH
A Concise Introduction to Thinking Visually

Jonathan S. Marion
Jerome W. Crowder

B L O O M S B U R Y

LONDON · NEW DELHI · NEW YORK · SYDNEY

Bloomsbury Academic
An imprint of Bloomsbury Publishing Plc

50 Bedford Square
London
WC1B 3DP
UK

175 Fifth Avenue
New York
NY 10010
USA

www.bloomsbury.com

First published 2013

British Library Cataloguing-in-Publication Data
A catalogue record for this book is available from the British Library.

ISBN: HB: 978-0-8578-5205-2
       PB: 978-0-8578-5206-9

Library of Congress Cataloging-in-Publication Data
A catalog record for this book is available from the Library of Congress.

Typeset by Apex CoVantage, LLC, Madison, WI, USA.
Printed and bound in Great Britain

CONTENTS

LIST OF TABLES AND ILLUSTRATIONS

Tables

Illustrations

ACKNOWLEDGEMENTS

There are many people who deserve thanks for their contributions and support in crafting this book. Our colleagues attending the Society for Visual Anthropology's annual Visual Research Conference, and our students—both on campus and in our workshops—have all contributed to our thinking about the issues at the heart of this text. The idea for this specific book first came up in a conversation between Jonathan Marion and Anna Wright (then an anthropology editor at Berg—now Bloomsbury) at the 2010 American Anthropological Association meeting in New Orleans; and we cannot thank her enough for her early enthusiasm and support for this project.

Because the ideas presented here are about visual research as it is broadly understood, we are especially appreciative of our colleagues who contributed glimpses into their own projects for the case studies in each chapter of this book: John Bishop, Elizabeth Cartwright, Jenny Chio, Kate Hennessy, Karen Nakamura, Sara Perry, Michele Reilly, Stephanie Takaragawa, Jennifer Wolowic, Terence Wright, and Anne Zeller. Stephanie Takaragawa and David Marion read the initial draft of this manuscript, and their early suggestions were invaluable in focusing our ongoing revisions. Likewise, feedback on the penultimate draft of the manuscript from Gavin Rose, Steve Moog, Terence Wright, and our anonymous reviewers all helped highlight areas in need of greater stylistic and theoretical clarification.

Especially considering that this book is about visual research, we greatly appreciate the aid of Joanna Cohan Scherer and the staff at the National Anthropological Archives, Ira Jacknis, Alicja Egbert, and Malcolm Collier, in identifying and securing the rights to the historical images in Chapters 2–4 (Figures 2.1, 2.2, 2.3, 3.1, and 4.2), and to Thomas DeFanti in providing us with a tour of the Calit2 facilities at University of California San Diego in April 2012, and then helping us secure the StarCAVE image in Chapter 7 through the timely assistance of Doug Ramsey (Figure 7.2). Chapter 6 would not be what it is today without Elizabeth Cartwright sharing her experiences using, making, and teaching about video research, or without the critical feedback from Michael Brims. More than anyone else, however, we are indebted to Michele Reilly, whose perspective as a digital archivist were both instrumental and invaluable in crafting Chapters 8 and 9, including the illustrative figures in these chapters.

We also want to thank two specific members of the Bloomsbury staff: Ian Buck for his incomparable assistance negotiating the editing and layout process, and

Louise Butler for her support bringing this project home. Our utmost gratitude also goes to Alicia Krouse for her continual support and understanding throughout the process of making this book a reality—if other authors could be so lucky. Finally, we must thank all of our research participants and collaborators who have allowed us into their lives, even—and especially—when we showed up with cameras in hand. It is only through their generosity that our own projects and thinking about visual research have and continue to develop.

CASE STUDY CONTRIBUTORS

John Bishop, Media Generation (United States)

- http://johnbishopexperience.com

Elizabeth Cartwright, Department of Anthropology, Idaho State University (United States)

- http://www.isu.edu/anthro/cartwright.shtml

Jenny Chio, Department of Anthropology, Emory University (United States)

- https://sites.google.com/site/jennytchio

Kate Hennessy, School of Active Arts and Technology, Simon Fraser University (Canada)

- http://hennessy.iat.sfu.ca

Karen Nakamura, Department of Anthropology, Yale University (United States)

- http://www.photoethnography.com

Sara Perry, Department of Archaeology, University of York (England)

- http://saraperry.wordpress.com

Michele Reilly, Head of Digital Service, University of Houston Libraries (United States)

- http://digital.lib.uh.edu

Stephanie Takaragawa, Department of Sociology, Chapman University (United States)

- http://www.chapman.edu/our-faculty/stephanie-takaragawa

Jennifer Wolowic, Department of Anthropology, University of British Columbia (Canada)

- http://blogs.ubc.ca/sumaxsaffect

Terence Wright, Art and Design Research Institute, University of Ulster (Northern Ireland)

- http://www.ulster.ac.uk/staff/t.wright.html

Anne Zeller, Anthropology Department, University of Waterloo (Canada)

- http://en.wikipedia.org/wiki/Anne_Zeller

INTRODUCTION

This introduction:

- Explains why this book was written
- Provides an overview of the structure and design features of this book
- Introduces the idea of thinking visually

Overview

While the need for a book like *Visual Research: A Concise Introduction to Thinking Visually* has existed for the past two decades within the social sciences, the rapid expansion of digital technologies has greatly increased this need. The capacity to take photos and video on handheld devices, and the ability to then store, post, and share such imagery online all offer tremendous opportunities for facilitating social research. The seemingly ever-present nature and availability of images enabled by digital technologies often masks the reality that they are all too often deployed with little technological proficiency, and even less theoretical and ethical consideration. Early uses of visual equipment were limited by their sheer size, cost, and need for specialized technical knowledge; this also meant that careful attention, planning, forethought, and judgment were involved in a way that is no longer required. Being able to shoot hours of digital footage or thousands of digital images from a handheld camera without changing film can be tremendously advantageous, but it also allows for far less critical awareness or attention than imposed by the limited nature of expensive media. This book bridges that gap by explaining how to take advantage of modern tools while thinking critically about all stages of image creation and dissemination, and by providing essential guidance for students and scholars embarking on almost any research project involving a visual dimension.

While almost all of the information we present has already appeared elsewhere, this information is typically (1) spread across numerous sources, and (2) written for other specialists, using concepts and language often inaccessible to newcomers. The most important ideas are often the least accessible to those who need this information the most. Unlike other texts, this book is written to familiarize the reader—that's you—with significant theoretical, methodological, ethical, and procedural considerations in a concise and highly accessible format. It is designed to be a one-stop guide for working with images that anyone interested in doing research on or with visual media will find extremely helpful. We explain key issues relating to how to use cameras in research (including both ethical and technical considerations) organized into short, focused chapters. *Visual Research: A Concise Introduction to Thinking Visually*, then, is a book for anyone wanting to learn how imagery—whether photos, video, or multimedia—can enhance their work.

We begin with a discussion of the ethics of making and using images. This is crucial to how researchers engage with the people around them and has important consequences for how images are taken, understood, used, and distributed. We emphasize that thinking about the ramifications of images *before* engaging in visual research is fundamental to capturing the most useful images—both literally and figuratively. Building on such considerations, the rest of this text is designed to help you think about and work with your own visual data, including creating, organizing, storing, and sharing it. Based on our experiences working with, producing, evaluating, and teaching about visual data,[1] we use examples from various professionals—highlighting the do's and do nots along with the why's and how's—to help you become a competent visual researcher and gain the understanding, experience, and proficiency to successfully integrate visuals into your own research. This book is *not* about teaching you how to do the visual research we have done, but rather uses our research to help you understand and accomplish the types of visual research that are best suited to your own work.

Focusing on broad ideas and the most common media (i.e., photography, video, and multimedia), we provide an overview and model that can be used for more specific and specialized domains (e.g., graphs, architecture, murals, paintings, etc.) without attempting to be all things to all people. This book is designed to provide you with significant theoretical, methodological, ethical, and procedural considerations in a concise, focused, and highly accessible format. We address basic concepts in order to make this text useful to students and readers from diverse personal, professional, and academic backgrounds. Our goal is to provide a broadly applicable way of thinking about and doing visual research rather than describing the numerous subtypes of such work. Ultimately then, you can expect this small book to create *big* changes in how you approach, think about, and implement visual methods in all of your fieldwork.

Design Features and Overall Structure

Based on our experiences working with, producing, evaluating, and teaching about visual data—and especially the Photography for the Field workshops we have taught at the American Anthropological Association (AAA) national meetings—we have designed and written this book to be a one-stop guide for working with images (whether video, photo, or multimedia), explaining key issues relating to how to actually use cameras in research, including both ethical and technical considerations. Key features and helpful tools include

- Bullet points at the start of each chapter stating the main ideas covered in that chapter.
- Brief case studies that complement each chapter—written by a wide array of international scholars (from Australia, Canada, England, Northern Ireland, and the United States) from various disciplines (e.g., anthropology, sociology, visual studies, and communications)—each illustrating specific issues, concerns, and considerations from their own work.
- Chapter summaries highlight how the basic concepts (e.g., perspective, exposure, framing, organization, etc.) can be applied across different fieldwork scenarios, with guides to further readings and resources.

In Section 1, Image Basics, we introduce the fundamental ideas involved in thinking visually, providing an overview of key issues and possibilities central to working with visual imagery. Since ethics are fundamental to *all* responsible social research, we begin this section with The Ethics of Images in Chapter 1, featuring a case study by Sara Perry, Director of Studies, Digital Heritage at the University of York (England). In Chapter 2, The Basics of Thinking Visually, we consider different models of thinking about and achieving "good" images, featuring a case study by U.S.-based documentary filmmaker and photographer John Bishop. Rounding out this section, Chapter 3, Thinking of Images as Data, outlines how to use images to ask—and answer—research questions, and features a case study by Canadian primatologist and visual anthropologist Anne Zeller.

Building on the concepts of the first section, Section 2—Making Images—is about *doing* visual research. Featuring a case study by U.S.-based visual anthropologist and filmmaker Karen Nakamura, Chapter 4 provides an overview of cameras in social science research, from film-based cameras to the implications of the now widespread availability and use of digital equipment. Chapters 5–7 deal with the advantages, disadvantages, and specific considerations of photography, video, and multimedia, respectively, featuring case studies by visual art scholar and photographer Terence Wright from the University of Ulster (Northern Ireland; Chapter 5), by participatory filmmaker Jennifer Wolowic from the University of British Columbia (Canada; Chapter 6), and anthropologist and new media artist Kate Hennessy from Simon Fraser University (Canada; Chapter 7).

Finally, Section 3, Using Images, explores and explains what to do with images in order to maximize their current and future research value. Chapter 8, Storage and Organization, explains how images are only truly useful when they can be managed to enhance research, and features a case study by University of Houston (United States) digital archivist Michele Reilly. Chapter 9, Exploring Images, explores how properly organized images can be revisited for a variety of uses, and

Figure 0.1   Art and Athleticism in Action: World and Blackpool Professional Latin Finalists, and U.S. National Professional Latin Champions, Maxim Kozhevnikov and Yulia Zagoruychenko are seen here competing (in the Team Match) at the 2007 Blackpool Dancesport Festival, in Blackpool, England. ©2007 Jonathan S. Marion. (Color original.)

Figure 0.2   Family at the Edge of the City: El Alto, Bolivia. ©1993 Jerome Crowder. (Color original.)

features a case study from Chapman University's (United States) Stephanie Takaragawa. Finally, Chapter 10, Using Images, features a case study from visual anthropologist Jenny Chio at Emory University (United States).[2]

The case studies featured in each chapter help highlight a crucial issue: There is no such thing as *"the* right way" to do visual research. As the range of case studies illustrates, context matters and equally strong visual research can look very different depending on topic, location, and approach. Equally important, however, is that across a broad range of contexts each case study also reflects careful attention to and consideration of the underlying issues involved. Although most of the authors' visual research has been done in very different settings and with very different people—Marion focusing on issues of performance, body, image, gender, and identity in the translocal culture and community of competitive ballroom dance (e.g., Marion 2008a, 2010, 2012; see Figure 0.1) and Crowder investigating urbanization and migration in the Bolivian and Peruvian Andes (e.g., Crowder 2003, 2006, 2007; see Figure 0.2)—we easily teach and write together. The underlying point is that the issues and ideas presented in these pages are neither a list of magical ingredients nor a set of paint-by-numbers guidelines for doing visual research. What this book does is provide you with a clear and concise introduction to key concepts and issues—from theoretical to the technical—involved in doing visual research. The book you are now reading is designed to show you how to start thinking visually so that you can design and do the research you want to do—in an ethical, informed, and productive manner.

Section 1

IMAGE BASICS

1

THE ETHICS OF IMAGES

In this chapter you will learn about:

- The importance of ethics for responsible research *and* for good research
- Seven key issues in visual ethics
- How these issues can be involved in very different types of research

Introducing Visual Ethics

More than just pretty (or ugly) pictures, images are among the most powerful communicative symbols. Not sure? Think about all the money spent on advertising campaigns in print, online, and on-screen (including televisions, tablets, and smart phones). Ask yourself why businesses pay hundreds of thousands of dollars to consultants, set designers, photographers, videographers, and other production personnel. Why do they pay over and over again to place these images in the public eye? It is because images have an impact. They convey meanings. Unlike narratives—which unfold progressively—images can present "everything" at once. This allows images to convey lots of information, including complex content and relationships, very quickly. Perhaps even more importantly, images can move us both more quickly and more powerfully, in ways that words alone may not (e.g., Barthes 1979/2010, Biella 2009, Bourdieu 2012, Douglas 2003, Sontag 2003).

Because images surround us, it is easy to overlook the work that goes into making and producing them—work that is always based on particular viewpoints. As responsible social scientists, however, it is vital to take into account the full range of ethical considerations and implications involved in making, using, and disseminating images. Because images always represent a particular view, images cannot accurately be seen as representing reality or truth. Just as we recognize what someone says as their opinion—whether research informants or researchers themselves—so too with the images they choose to produce. Just as you have to decide what questions to ask in an interview, you also have to decide which images to create, produce, or select. Just as you choose particular quotes and where to place them, so too with images.

The keys to doing good social research are (1) having clear research questions and (2) choosing research methods appropriate to answering these questions. Ultimately, this book is designed to help you do just that. Later chapters will help you decide what types of visual data and organization will be the most useful in your work. Before we start dealing with larger theoretical and practical concerns however, we want to discuss the most important idea in conducting good social research: ETHICS COME FIRST. Regardless of any other consideration, we have obligations to those we work with, and these must take precedence over getting the best shot or any other such choices. In the long run, however, ethical research also usually ends up being the best research.

Here is an example: Imagine you are doing research on a religious ceremony and you think that visual data may provide helpful documentation, but the ceremony is not supposed to be photographed. Some of you may think about all the microcameras available—the spy-style still and video cameras designed to look like key chains and pens—and how you could get such devices into sensitive ceremonies, secure areas, or private meetings where a larger camera would never be allowed. But at what cost? You have violated people's trust and contemptuously disregarded their wishes. Maybe they never find out, but that certainly does not make it right. At best, you will not be able to talk about the images with your informants and have them explained by the participants themselves (more on photo elicitation in Chapter 10). And what if you are caught? You have lost people's trust, probably have destroyed possibilities for future research, and may in fact have lost your welcome in the community altogether. Your camera could be confiscated, if not destroyed, and you may be threatened or even physically assaulted. And for what?

Now imagine that you followed people's wishes and clearly kept all cameras far from the ceremony. In this scenario, people continue to answer your questions, and in all likelihood, may feel that they can trust you that much more. When people learn that they can trust you—over time and across various situations—the most interesting data emerges. Building rapport is crucial to social research; no image is worth more than building and maintaining good rapport. Careful consideration of people (and other living things) involved in our research projects and settings is the right thing to do. As the proverbial frosting on the cake, however, it also typically facilitates the best research (see Figure 1.1).

Things can get much more complicated in real world research. What if you are working in a community, but instead of being unanimously told *not* to photograph or video a religious ceremony, one group wants you to and one does not? What if one group has more religious authority, more political authority, or greater financial resources than the other? What if one group is hosting you? What if you are doing contract work and the funding organization wants something different? Deciding

Figure 1.1 **Rapport:** U.S. Professional Rhythm National Semifinalists at the time, this image shows F.J. and Catherine Abaya at home shortly after having competed at the 2004 Seattle Star Ball. The rapport and trust built over years earned the photographer access to record this post-competition reward of downtime for the Abayas. They spent this time in front of the television with their dogs . . . and with two -dozen donuts, earned through three weeks of strict dieting and extra practices leading up to the competition. ©2004 Jonathan S. Marion. (Color original.)

what to do in such situations is often difficult precisely because there can be competing legitimate perspectives and values. While there cannot be any one-size-fits-all solution to such complex situations, there are many helpful resources available, such as the codes of ethics produced by organizations like the American Anthropological Association, the American Sociological Association, and the International Visual Sociology Association. Some of these resources are more specific to working with visual data than others, but all provide useful guidelines for thinking through the complex issues involved.[1]

Seven Key Issues in Visual Ethics

We use the term *visual ethics* not to differentiate these from other ethical considerations, but to show you how ethical principles apply to working with visual materials and data. To provide a basic example: Think about recording audio and writing down the content of an interview or a political speech. How could you keep the identity of these people confidential? Think about photographing or video recording the same interview or political speech. Now how could you keep identities confidential? The point is that the same ethical principles may involve different considerations when working with visual data, and that these considerations are important to think about at all stages of the research process, from design to implementation to dissemination.

The following seven issues represent what we believe to be the key ethical considerations in visual research. As you read and think about these issues, it is important to keep in mind that this is not an ingredient list for ethical research. It is not a recipe you can simply follow. Rather, each of these items is an issue for you to carefully consider as it relates to your own research and the relevant parties. We follow the presentation of these key issues with an illustrative example and a related case study.

1. *Representational authority.* Who controls the perspectives from which images are created? Should researchers get to decide how they depict those they work with? Should it be up to those represented in the images? What about interested audiences (such as funding agencies, or the oft-cited public's right to know)? Such choices involve a triadic research relationship between three groups: researchers, subjects/participants, and audiences (Crawford and Simonsen 1992: 3). And each of these groups may contain a range of perspectives. Should you, as the researcher, get to decide how to depict something about a group of people or a particular site? Should the people themselves get to decide, regardless of your research goals? Does an outside public (such as a research sponsor) have the right to choose which people and activities get recorded and which do not?

2. *Decontextualization/circulation of images (and the problem of lack of control).* Once you have created an image, (a) how and where does it get used, and (b) who has control over those decisions? If you post something on a research-specific website, who has access? If it is only presented to a limited audience, what about ethical guidelines on the importance of publicizing research findings? If publicly posted, what about outside parties who can now copy and disseminate images that could be personal, private, or even sacred? What about the fact that such further circulation and use of images may well take place out of context?[2]

3. *Presumed versus actual outcomes of image display.* Because images can be perceived differently by viewers, they can generate different outcomes than originally intended. Before using an image—whether as part of the research or in the reporting process—try and step away from how you think about and see an image, and ask how others *could* see the same image. How might friends of those depicted view it? How about family members, political rivals, or enemies? What if an audience misses your intended point? What if people with a different background do not *see* the same nuances you do, and focus instead on what they consider unenlightened, superficial, or even barbaric practices? What if the people involved in your research see themselves as being ridiculed? What if outside viewers see your images as confirming their beliefs about "less developed" foreigners, the impoverished, or the disenfranchised?

6

4. *Relations with and responsibilities toward research subjects/communities.* We all begin research with particular agendas, usually to answer specific sets of questions. Getting answers, however, is not the only or even the most important consideration in the field. Rather, because we are working with human subjects (or even non-human subjects, such as Zeller's case study in Chapter 3) we have responsibilities to them that must come first. As noted earlier, taking the wishes of research subjects and communities into account helps maintain good rapport both for current research and for future researchers. Even if this is not the case, why should our own academic projects trump the wishes of others? We are talking about other people's lives, and it is important to remember that the repercussions of our actions can last long after we leave the field.

5. *Balancing privacy versus publicity, depending on subjects' wishes.* One tenet of ethical research is to publicize research work and findings, rather than hoarding such knowledge for one's self. At the same time, some information can be sensitive, whether for personal, professional, or other reasons. Whether it is to protect confidential data, avoid embarrassment, or respect others' sacred beliefs, the decisions we make about reporting our research findings need to be informed by careful consideration and respect for the subjects' wishes.

6. *The importance of communication with and consent of subjects and communities at every stage of the research process.* While the idea of **informed consent** is fairly well established among researchers in the social sciences, it is critical to remember that research subjects typically do not have the same academic background that you do. "So what?" you may ask, "As long as they consent isn't that good enough?". In a word: No. Do they understand how, where, and why their images will be used? Do they understand who will have access to these images? If not, their consent is not *informed*. Do your subjects realize that they can say "no" to you without adverse consequences? What if your subject's culture considers it improper or hostile to deny a request? And what if people allow you to take pictures of them at work or with their family, but then change their mind? Do they understand that they can withdraw their consent on the spot, after a night's sleep and consideration, the next week, or even later? Once you know what images you plan to use, and in what ways, have you informed your subjects and confirmed that you still have their consent? What about people who insist on you using an image that you would prefer not to use?

7. *The collection and dissemination of visual materials within the context of globally expanding media savvy and presence.* The previous six issues need to be considered in light of modern technology and circumstances. Photos and video footage from years past were typically published on the other side of the planet and in a completely foreign language from the people they depicted.[3] With Internet access, however, people now can access a vast range of materials. The ever-expanding awareness of and access to the Internet may have significant repercussions that you must think about as part of conducting responsible research.

Sometimes it is easy to know what is the right (or wrong) thing to do. Most of the time real life situations are more complicated, meaning that these issues will play out differently in various situations and contexts. Rather than just reiterating the importance of these ethical considerations, here are some concrete examples of how the considerations described above have played out in real research.

Ethics in Action

Marion's study of competitive ballroom dancers demonstrates that image matters in many ways (e.g., Marion 2008a). More precisely, the dancers' competitive success is ultimately based on the image they portray. Although the activity is physical, competitions are judged visually. Dancers, therefore, care a great deal about how they are depicted and portrayed. It was specifically because the visual element of ballroom culture is so important to the dancers that Marion started thinking about and pursuing visual anthropology. As Marion has pointed out elsewhere (2010), photography provided him with a recognized and valued role within the ballroom world, thereby facilitating his research. At the same time, precisely because dancers' images are so significant, Marion had to evaluate a variety of ethical considerations in his research. In preparing the images for sociologist Julia Ericksen's (2011) book, for instance, the image originally chosen for the cover had to be replaced with an image preferred by the couple depicted (Issue 1). Similarly, while Marion received explicit permission to take photographs at the studios and competitions described in Ericksen's book, specific people chose not to be photographed at one studio, and those depicted in each image also gave explicit permission for each image before the images were published (Issue 6).[4]

Visual research on competitive ballroom dancing presents other challenges. What should Marion do when he wants to use an image to help explain mistakes or point out things dancers might not want associated with their image? While each specific situation is different, in light of intersecting considerations (Issues 2, 4, 5, and 7), Marion's working rule of thumb has been twofold:

1. Do not publish images (either in print or online) when (a) people can be identified, and (b) the researcher cannot control access to the image.
2. Only use images in classroom or conference presentations when (a) dancers are unlikely to be recognized (thus helping maintain anonymity), and (b) audiences do not have access to the images after their presentation.

Ultimately, however, ethics matter for one very simple reason: *Images have consequences*. Whether you are sharing images with a colleague for a conference paper or publication, posting an image online, or including them in your own work, there can be serious and significant consequences. The most telling example of the enduring ethical implications and responsibilities of working with visual media from Marion's research concerns Larinda McRaven, a four-time U.S. National

Professional Open Smooth Finalist with partner Steven Hevenor. Having already known Larinda through Dance-Forums.com where both were staff members, Marion interviewed her and Steven in June 2004 at the Yankee Classic in Boston, Massachusetts.

Arriving in Hollywood Beach, Florida for the 2005 United States Dancesport Championships, Marion received an e-mail from the Hartford *Courant*, Larinda and Steven's local newspaper, that asked for images to use in a story about the couple. Thinking that he was doing them a favor and partially paying them back for their interview, Marion e-mailed the newspaper one of the few images he had on his laptop in Florida. Waking up the next morning, Marion learned that his image accompanied the front-page story "Assault Claim Divides Dancers." While Larinda remains a friend to this day, that was a powerful lesson for Marion about carefully considering the actual outcomes of how his images are used and viewed (Issue 3 primarily, but also 1, 2, and 4). While we all make mistakes—and this was a major one on his part—because Marion has been careful about how his images get used, dancers have continued to let him bring his camera behind the scenes and to trust him as an anthropologist, a photographer, and a friend. In short—and as pointed out earlier in this chapter—ethical research produces good research.

ARCHAEOLOGICAL IMAGERY AND THE ETHICS OF VISUAL REPRESENTATION

Sara Perry—University of York, England

I am an archaeological anthropologist who, like all anthropologists, works with a range of visual media on a daily basis. These media include everything from the most innocuous-seeming of line graphs to photos, videos, maps, artifact displays, illustrations, charts, and related digital and analog renderings.

In addition to making such visuals, I have spent multiple years studying the images that archaeologists and other practitioners use to populate their scholarly outputs. Despite the innovation that often characterizes visual production in archaeology—perhaps most obvious in high-resolution modeling of, and virtual engagement with, sites—rarely is such production subject to critical interrogation. At best, this means that archaeological pictures are regularly used as little more than facile, unacknowledged, descriptive devices. At worst, it means that the longstanding historical injustices of our disciplinary practices can be found congealed in our visual representations.

For example, in the context of an analysis of over sixty images accompanying publications on prehistoric colonization activities (most intended for academic audiences), the majority were reproduced without any authorial credit whatsoever (Perry 2006, 2009), or else such credit amounted to near-illegible or unidentifiable sets of initials inscribed along the border of the image. Many pictures collapsed peopling activity into outmoded, iconographic tropes, erroneously representing it as a man-only pursuit of mammoths or a seemingly intentional program of global domination (e.g., Figure 1.2, top). In especially dubious fashion, photographs of *modern* Aboriginal peoples were commonly appropriated as stand-ins for prehistoric colonizers, reducing them to ethnographic anachronisms.

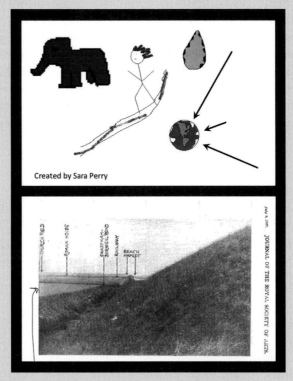

Created by Sara Perry

Figure 1.2 Constructedness of Images: TOP: Perry's own remediated interpretation of the common iconographic elements used to depict archaeological colonization events. Perry's crudely drawn renderings are no more legitimate or academically sound than those that populate most professional publications on the topic. But here, at least, she identifies herself as their originator and, in so doing, takes responsibility for their implications. BOTTOM: Image excerpt from Perry's Ph.D. dissertation, which uses multiple layers of annotation (drawing on the image itself) and self-reference (in the caption) to disrupt simplistic interpretation of the visual object. This image is reproduced in Wheeler (1927) and then again by Perry (2011), although the original creator and annotator are unidentified. (Color originals.)

To reproduce these pictures here—unmediated—would be to perpetuate the very questionable practices of visualization that I seek to dismantle. What is critical, however, is that in their original publication, many of our fundamental standards of academic integrity—not to mention critical scholarship—were disregarded. Not only were unsubstantiated, prejudicial arguments enshrined in the images, but the makers and commissioners of those images were left untraceable.

My response to such a predicament has been to articulate basic principles of practice for everyday image use. These principles entail little more than legibly attributing authorship to all visual media; annotating or reflectively manipulating such media to signal their constructedness (Figure 1.2, top and bottom); demanding that, as per text, they be subject to blatant critical analysis in our scholarly book and peer review processes; and publishing clear image bibliographies to accompany all of our outputs. Such recommendations are no more onerous than those applied to textual media and, indeed, should surely now be a requirement of rigorous scholarship.

Summary

We started with ethics because ethics must always come first. Ethical considerations are essential both for doing responsible research *and* for doing good research. Next, we identified the following seven key issues for working with visual data:

1. Negotiating representational authority, including the triadic research relationship between researchers, subjects, and audiences.
2. The decontextualization/circulation of images (and the problem of lack of control).
3. Presumed versus actual outcomes of image display.
4. Relations with and responsibilities toward research subjects/communities.
5. Balancing privacy versus publicity (depending on subjects' wishes).
6. The importance of communication with and consent of subjects/communities at every stage of the research process.
7. The collection and dissemination of visual materials within the context of globally expanding media savvy and presence.

Recognizing that these are not steps to be followed, but issues to be thought about and addressed, we presented an example from Marion's work and a case study by Sara Perry, highlighting how the concepts involved are applied across different fieldwork scenarios. Ideally, you should think through the ethical issues of your own research as you are designing your project—that is, before you ever start—but always remember to revisit these issues as your research progresses, complications crop up, and new issues arise. Three particularly important resources you can consult as you continue to work with these issues are in the following section.

- Code of Ethics of the American Anthropological Association (February 2009)
  - www.aaanet.org/issues/policy-advocacy/upload/Code-of-Ethics.cfm
- International Visual Sociology Association (IVSA) Code of Research Ethics and Guideline
  - Papademas, Diana and the International Visual Sociology Association (2009), "IVSA Code of Research Ethics and Guidelines," *Visual Studies*, 24/3: 250–57.
- Statement of Ethical Practice for the British Sociological Association—Visual Sociology Group (December 2006)
  - www.visualsociology.org.uk/about/ethical_statement.php

2

STARTING TO THINK VISUALLY

In this chapter you will learn about:

- Different approaches to working with and using images—such as photojournalism, art, and ethnography—and some of their histories and differences
- The vocabulary of images (e.g., framing, composition, angles, lighting) and how these elements fit together
- What makes a good (research) image

Introducing Visual Literacy

As you read through the rest of the materials in this book, we want to emphasize the idea of *visual literacy* and the overall importance of thinking visually in the social sciences. John Debes coined the term visual literacy in 1969. It refers to a person's overall competence in discerning and interpreting visual cues, from symbols to behavior, that lie at the heart of all visual learning and communication (Debes 1969: 27). Despite the ongoing bombardment of visual images online, in television, movies, and print media, all too often researchers are not trained to critically think about the images they see, let alone how to use visual media as part of their research. This is particularly unfortunate since access to less expensive and more portable digital photography and video recording devices often means that more and more researchers can "snap some shots" or "get some footage" as part of their research; but they do so with little forethought and without any clear understanding of imagery or image making. That is one reason we wrote this book: to help you—the reader—think through, understand, and incorporate visual research most usefully into your own work and interests.

Different Approaches to Working with and Using Images

The old adage that "a picture is worth a thousand words" is part of the advantage of thinking about and working with images as data (the topic of Chapter 3). At the same time, this is also the challenge of working with images: Images can communicate so much because what (i.e., how much) they can communicate is often quite open-ended.[1] Think about a flag for a minute. Which flag did you choose? Would everyone else choose the same flag? More importantly, would the flag you chose mean the same thing to you as it does to everyone else?

What about a dog? It could be seen as a pet, a companion, a protector, a threat, a weapon, or a food—to name a few possibilities. Everyone does not see the same image of a dog as the same *thing*. But what each person does see is not random. It is based on a particular perspective. Some of this perspective comes from each person's own history and background, but a lot of culture comes from how something is shown.

For example, what if the image was of a big, snarling dog? Is the dog filling the whole image area or is it farther away? Are its eyes looking toward the camera or somewhere else in the frame? Is the dog at eye-level, just above us, or far below us? Is it in a field of flowers or a junkyard? Similarly, what is the nature of the image itself? Is it realistic, impressionistic, black-and-white, or color? Is it, a painting, a photograph, or a video? Is the image in a newspaper, on a website, or in an art gallery? Is it on thin, grainy paper, photo paper, canvas, online, projection, liquid crystal display, or plasma screen? Is it an image in a book, in a film, on a boardroom wall, or on a billboard? Is it in a frame and, if so, what color is the frame and is the frame made of wood, metal, or plastic? Is the image presented on its own or with other images (and if so, what other images)? Is there any additional context or captioning? The point here is that images can be made and presented in lots of different ways. We thus want to differentiate between three of the more recognized models of working with and using images—photojournalism, art, and ethnography—and how these approaches think about and use images.

Photojournalism

The hallmark of photojournalism is the timely and accurate illustration of current news events. Although they shared early roots (e.g., Riis 1890/1997), we view photojournalism as somewhat different from documentary photography (which typically involves a more longitudinal approach, and is rooted in social activism[2]). Strongly influenced by technological developments, modern photojournalism can be said to have started in the mid-1930s with the introduction of the 35mm camera (the easily portable Leica). For the first time photographers were able to go wherever the story was, and follow unfolding events. Newspapers and news magazines (e.g., *LIFE Magazine*) started relying on timely images to illustrate current events, often including prominent image-based (versus text-based) news stories. Eminent photojournalists of the day became household names. The Magnum agency was founded in 1947 in order to represent photojournalists' interests (such as retaining copyrights of their own images). The deep legacy and current impact of photojournalism are clear: Images are expected for and integral to any major news story today.

By far the most popular form of photojournalism with an ethnographic bent today is *National Geographic Magazine*.[3] In line with other photojournalism, *National Geographic* is about telling stories in a few very "good" photos; in fact, their reputation is built upon their strong images. Remember though, their purpose is primarily to sell magazines, and they use images that may objectify their subjects without completely telling the entire story.[4] Additionally, professional writers usually write the articles, and they may not even accompany the photographer on the assignment.

Art

Where photojournalism focuses on accuracy, art represents the "nonutilitarian elaboration of a thing or act" (Heider 2007: 124): any elements of an act or object that do not contribute to its functionality are its artistic components. Art is not concerned with accuracy alone; it invites and welcomes interpretation. In other words, the artist's perspective is not essential to appreciating art; what the audience brings to art is part of the exchange.[5] Exchange is a key concept here because, if anything, art effuses intent. Subtle or dramatic, exchange is always present. Like all forms of expression, art uses the camera to capture and distort (in the loosest sense) details in order to help us rethink assumptions and social ideas. Artists make personal comments on life and society, and those who use cameras choose to do so for a variety of reasons, including reproducibility, distribution, accuracy, accessibility, and expense.

Ethnography

Photography has a long history in anthropology (e.g., Edwards 1994). Franz Boas, widely regarded as the father of American anthropology, used both photography and film as part of his fieldwork with Kwakwaka'wakw (then known as the Kwakiutl) starting in 1894 (Jacknis 1984). Unlike art historians' studies *of* images—and as the work of Boas already demonstrated—ethnography uses images as both (a) a means of study and (b) a means of (re)presentation. In 1896, Félix-Louis Regnault used film to begin a cross-cultural study of movement; and in 1898, Alfred Haddon used video as part of the Torres Straits Expedition. In 1914 Edward Curtis produced *In the Land of the Head Hunters* (since renamed *In the Land of the War Canoes*), which served as a model for the first feature-length documentary, Robert Flaherty's 1922 film *Nanook of the North*. The work of Bateson and Mead in Bali and New Guinea is probably the best-known and most comprehensive early use of photography

Figure 2.1 Self-Portrait: This image, taken in Picuris, New Mexico, in 1957 is an excellent example of a creative means for photographing cultural material that is both an aesthetically pleasing portrait and ethnographically rich image (i.e., chock-full of ethnographic information, providing much potential for further inquiry). This photograph was made as part of longer series of cultural inventories of homes in the area, part of a study of Picuris Pueblo carried out by the late Dr. Bernard Siegel of Stanford University. These recordings of home interiors were a more systematic evolution of the earlier FSA/OWI (Farm Security Administration/Office of War Information) images of homes. Photo by John Collier, Jr. (r7138). (Black-and-white original.)

(Bateson and Mead 1942) and video (e.g., Bateson and Mead 1952, 1954a, 1954b) in true ethnographic research. Despite such early and important precedents, photography remained under-theorized and underutilized in mainstream anthropology, with film, and then video, receiving somewhat more widespread appreciation in the other social sciences.

Since Section 2 of this book, Making Images, provides more specifics regarding cameras in social science research, what is most important here is to recognize what has differentiated ethnographic image use from other approaches (such as photojournalism and art): a commitment to embedded research and the use of visual media as part of generating—and only then presenting—deeper and more nuanced research. What should be clear at this point is that images do not simply show any one thing; and that different approaches to imagery are based on different values and genres. In all cases, however, there are visual codes that color our viewing of an image.[6]

Of course, there is not an indelible line that separates photography and film from photojournalism or ethnography. Very strong ethnographic images, for instance, are considered artistic because of their composition and ability to relate a feeling or commentary. Likewise, art photos or films can share documentary characteristics, even while rooted in social commentary or personal expression (see, for example, Figures 2.1, 2.2, and 2.3).

The Vocabulary of an Image

Mise-en-scène is a term taken from theatre and film production that refers to the complete spatial organization of the image, including framing, composition, angle, lighting, and perspective. There are numerous books and articles available about each of these topics,[7] and while we will revisit some key considerations in Chapters 5 and 6, our main purpose here is to help you start *recognizing* and *thinking* about these elements in the images you see and create. For y/our purposes then, let us to start with some very basic definitions:

- **Framing:** what shows up in the image, that is, what actually appears in the viewfinder or frame (Figure 2.4)
- **Composition:** the arrangement of objects within an image's framing (Figure 2.5)
- **Angle / Perspective:** position of the camera relative to the subject, such as straight on, from the side, eye level, below, or above the subject, and so forth. (Figure 2.5)
- **Lighting:** the amount, source, and location of light sources in an image (Figure 2.6)

Of course while each of these elements can be significant on its own, it is the *gestalt* of these elements—how they integrate with each other—that the viewer sees as the image.

Figure 2.2　Girl Dancing: Both this image and Figure 2.3 demonstrate the multiplicity of approaches images can take-on. This image, taken in Vicos, Perú, is strong because the subject fills the frame due to its low angle, and creates a strong sense of energy and movement. It also includes a great deal of ethnographic information, including clothing, behavior, skills, interactions, and the new school building in background. At one level it could be considered photojournalism as it concisely tells a story within one frame, but also art as well as ethnographic due to its composition and content. Photo by Mary E.T. Collier, 1955 (n10353–3252–5d). (Black-and-white original.)

Additional Dimensions

Additional considerations in viewing and understanding images are the dimensions of exposure, contrast, and the media involved in making an image. At the most fundamental level, **exposure** refers to the amount of light captured (and thus shown) in an image. The brightest parts of an image are the **highlights,** the darkest parts are the **shadows,** and **contrast** is the range between an image's highlights and shadows. While many believe an observer's attention first goes to the brightest part of an image, in fact it goes to the areas of greatest contrast. You may notice this most easily in black and white images, but examine any image carefully and you will soon see that this is part of how we view images (for example, consider Figure 2.6). This is worth remembering both for understanding why you notice some elements of an image before others, and also when designing your own images. One other general consideration that we will return to in Chapter 5 is **depth of field,** the portion of the image from foreground to background that is within acceptable focus.

Figure 2.3 Woman in Home with Portraits: This intriguing image, taken in Peñasco, New Mexico, uses the rule of thirds (see Chapter 5) to bring various subjects into relation with each other while being in an intimate setting. The image is ethnographically rich as well, with content on material culture, economics, technology, dress, cultural aesthetics, and a very rich potential for use in photo elicitation. Photo by John Collier, Jr., 1943 (r0594, also LC-USW3–013688-C). (Black-and-white original.)

What Makes a Good Image?

With a basic vocabulary for thinking about images, we come to the key question: What makes a good image? The answer is simple: It depends. As discussed above, photojournalism, art, and ethnography are three approaches (of many), each of which uses images to accomplish different things. Evaluating what makes one image better than another thus depends on its intended purposes. Here we want to stress that, for the purposes of social research, we feel that the best images are those that best tell the story. This is where ethnographic understanding (knowing what's going on) comes into play by informing the intent and impact of ethnographic images. It is by paying attention to and participating in the lives around you that you will start to know and understand where to be with your camera—still or video—and how to best capture a particular story or illustrative moment.

Indeed, as social researchers the purpose of developing technical and artistic skills is to best represent the lived reality of those with whom we work.[8] This task

19

Figure 2.4 Framing: Salome washes her family's clothes in the patio of their house in El Alto, Bolivia. The top image is shot at a focal length of 16mm (on a full-frame DSLR), while the bottom image is shot at a focal length of 35mm. Wide angles are excellent for establishing shots and providing context, and while both of these images are made with wide angles, the distance to the subject determines just how much context is captured in each photograph. Both images are taken from the same location, with the same equipment. ©2011 Jerome Crowder. (Color originals.)

Figure 2.5 Composition and **Angle/Perspective:** U.S. Professional 9-Dance Champions Peter and Alexandra Perzhu, seen here competing at the 2011 United States Dancesport Championships in Orlando, Florida. While both images show the exact same element in the Perzhus' Cha-Cha routine, the **composition** on the left is much busier, with several other couples, judges, and audience. Likewise, from this **angle/perspective** Alexandra's body blocks most of Peter, and the three-dimensional shapes made by both cannot be seen. The **angle/perspective** of the image on the right, however, depicts the Perzhus' dynamic positions, while the **composition** largely isolates the Perzhus against the floor while still showing other couples in the background. ©2011 Jonathan S. Marion. (Color originals.)

is the same as for any ethnographic project, but the tools—and thus the potentials for (and limits to) understanding—are different when working with audio-visual media. To reiterate, the best ethnographic imagery (from photographs to films to multimedia) comes from cultural knowledge and understanding. From this, you—as the media-maker—decide on the intent and message of an image, and then utilize the vocabulary of an image to convey what you have decided is the story that should be understood and appreciated.

Certainly what makes a *good* image is as technical as it is cultural, both in its intent as well as interpretation.[9] Commonly referred to as the *ethnographic triad* (Crawford and Simonsen 1992; also see Scherer 1990, Ruby 2000), there is a triangular relationship between ethnographer, participants, and audience. Whom the ethnographer is shooting for (or thinks will see the images) affects subject and framing choices. Likewise, participants' relationship with the ethnographer affects the intimacy between the two, which manifests in different types of images. The third

---

21

Figure 2.6 Lighting (Ambient versus Flash): Luis builds a door inside his uncle's carpentry shop, located in the Urbanization Bautista Saavedra, El Alto, Bolivia. The top image is exposed with available (ambient) light, while the lower image benefits from the flash filling in the shadows. ©2011 Jerome Crowder. (Color originals.)

leg of this relationship, between audience and participant, involves whether partici-pants understand how their images will be made and used.[10] All of these relation-ships affect the way we understand what makes up a "good" image (and whether there is an agreed aesthetic to it or not).

Marion confronts these differences when showing images to dancers, judges, audience members, academic students and colleagues, as well as other photogra-phers. Crowder's images are scrutinized by some Bolivians for showing the poverty and not the beauty of the country, or relying too much on a narrative produced by American art photographers. Each viewer brings a set of personal preferences that may or may not coincide with those of other audience members. If you feel that your image conveys knowledge about a culture or moves someone to understand a situation differently, then chances are you have a good photo. (Besides, there will always be someone to tell you how to improve it—guaranteed!)

One thing we want to stress here is that "knowing what's going on" can mean many things. In some settings or cases it may simply be having a feeling that some-thing is amiss or about to happen. In such cases, make sure your lens cap is off, and that your camera is on and set to the current lighting conditions. From there, just go with your intuition and your knowledge of the people and patterns around you (as much as you can do so within the ethical guidelines laid out in Chapter 1). John Bishop's case study in this chapter describes exactly this dynamic, where technical considerations and the ability to evoke cultural insight and understanding emerge as the fundamental purpose of ethnographic imagery.

VISUAL EXPERIENCE ON THE MOVE

John Melville Bishop—Media-Generation, United States

I shoot people doing things, events that can neither be predicted nor repeated. Early in my career as a filmmaker and photographer, I learned to trust my eyes and body to move subconsciously into compositions that the situation demanded and build stories on a visual logic. Rather than think about formal protocols or rules about how and what to shoot, my goal was to have the camera disappear and be responsive to the moment. In media terms, if I do not shoot it well, it might as well not have happened.

For *Choose Life* (about a nuclear freeze demonstration), I shot a sit-in with the cover-age expected of a professional cameraman (a series of wide, medium, and close-up shots). Then the director suggested I sit down with the demonstrators. Suddenly the camera went from being an observer to a participant. The camera was at risk; I was

Figure 2.7 The Camera in the Action: When the camera is immersed in the event, the story unfolds within the field of view. "If you are press, you belong on the other side of the fence and get there right now," the officer tells the camera, held by Bishop, who is next in line to be busted. Film frames from *Choose Life,* a film by John Bishop and Robbie Leppzer.

at risk. A series of compositions unfolded in a continuous shot as the people ahead of me were arrested and carried out, until I was next in line. A policeman leaned down and said, "If you're press, you belong on the other side of the fence." It was a breakthrough for me to be both in the event and filming it, and to see the contrast in the footage of the two approaches.

A single shot that evolves is more evocative than an edited sequence, but sometimes you do not have that option. And as an editor, a part of my mind while shooting is on the story I am telling and whether I am getting the footage to tell that story. In *Himalayan Herders* (an ethnographic portrait of a Nepalese village), we had one chance to film a capture marriage in which a girl is grabbed by a boy and his friends. I gathered with the groom's friends before dawn at the bride's house. All I knew was that it would happen fast and move from a tight cluster of houses across 200 yards of terraced fields to the groom's house. I had to concentrate not only on being in the moment, but also on a logical sequence of shots to convey the spatial and symbolic geometry of the bride going from her father's to her father-in-law's house. As she was grabbed, I started filming from within the group and followed her through the narrow alleys between houses. I paused as the group passed with the village (and the groom's house) in the background, then ran ahead of the group to get them approaching (with the mountains and the bride's house behind). As they surrounded me, I walked with them through the narrow gate to the courtyard, as one of the participants. The whole thing took three minutes and is in the film as it was shot. The audience experiences exactly what I experienced.

In other settings, this same goal of culturally informed insight can best if not only be achieved by *previsioning*[11] the image—by imagining the picture as you want it to appear in advance, thereby allowing you to be (1) in the right place, (2) at the right time, and (3) with the right equipment and settings. Take, for example, the image in Figure 2.8, Marion's most widely circulated and published image.[12] Taken at the 2005 Embassy Ball in Irvine, California, this picture shows the signature scissor-kick in the opening pass of Dominico Soale and Gioia Cerosoli's quickstep routine. The reigning World and Blackpool Amateur Ballroom Champions at the time, Dominico and Gioia are an Italian couple that Marion saw twice a year at most: once at the Embassy Ball in Irvine, California and once at the British Open Championships in Blackpool, England. It took Marion three years (with attempts on six occasions) to finally capture this image.

Beyond the obvious difficulties of composing and capturing Dominico and Gioia mid-flight, Marion had to contend with such obstacles as (1) at least five other couples dancing on the floor simultaneously; (2) judges standing around the edges of the floor; (3) the limited vantage points available amidst the spectators' seats and tables; and (4) that this scissor-kick took place around two-thirds to three-quarters

Figure 2.8 Previsioning: This image shows Dominico Soale and Gioia Cerosoli's signature scissor-kick opening to their quickstep routine at the 2005 Embassy Ball Dancesport Championships, Irvine, California. This is the type of image that depends on previsioning based on ethnographic understanding. ©2005 Jonathan S. Marion. (Color original.)

of the way down the side of the ballroom floor, and on opposite sides of the floor in different rounds.

Having seen Dominico and Gioia perform this element in their routine, Marion could imagine the shot he wanted. By previsioning the image—being able to imagine what he wanted it to look like—Marion could position himself accordingly, and have all of the settings on his camera ready to maximize his chance of getting the image he was "hunting."

This photo for Marion and Figure 5.6 for Crowder have both been widely recognized as good pictures, and as photographers we are pleased to have our technical and artistic efforts recognized. As visual anthropologists, however, we are more concerned with crafting images that tell a good ethnographic story. Attention and respect, especially over time, facilitate the rapport and understanding of (a) what stories to tell and (b) which images best tell these stories. It is this topic—thinking of images as data—to which we turn in Chapter 3.

Summary

This chapter started by introducing photojournalism, art, and ethnography as three (of many) approaches to working with and using images based in different histories and with different (if sometimes overlapping) objectives. Next, we (1) explored the vocabulary of images, including issues such as framing, composition, angle, lighting, and perspective, and (2) then looked at how these considerations mesh with each other to produce an image. Finally, we addressed what makes a "good" ethnographic image, focusing on how ethnographic understanding (i.e., knowing what's going on) influences and informs ethnographic image making.

Further Readings and Resources

- *Appropriating Images: The Semiotics of Visual Representation* (Tomaselli 1996)
- *Photographic Composition: A Visual Guide* (Zakia and Page 2011)
  - See, especially, the "looking" exercises at the end of most chapters.
- *Visual Methodologies: An Introduction to the Interpretation of Visual Materials* (Rose 2007)

3

THINKING OF IMAGES AS DATA

In this chapter you will learn about:

- How to use images to ask and answer research questions
- How images illustrate, explain, and evoke understandings differently than text
- How thinking of and treating images as data facilitates analyzing images for meaning and understanding

Introducing Images as Data

Having discussed the ethics of making and working with imagery in Chapter 1 and then having looked at the basics of thinking visually in Chapter 2, this chapter outlines how to use images to systematically ask and answer research questions. A key consideration is to start thinking of images as more than illustrations, and as data in their own right. Imagine that you are doing research on a social movement, a medical situation, a religious ceremony, an environmental conflict, or any other such issue. How do you collect data? In most fieldwork settings it will involve some combination of observations, interviews, and participation. But how do these data actually get recorded? Most of the time, data get recorded through *written* field notes (or printed transcripts of recorded interviews). Certainly these notes can be used as the basis for descriptions that illustrate a situation, an issue, a process, a phenomenon, or even a thought process. The notes themselves are data, but it is only from a broader, contextually-informed perspective that you, as the researcher, can decide which materials best tell the outsider what is going on.

We are suggesting that you start thinking of images in a parallel manner: as *visual* field notes. Just like any other field notes, the images you generate from observations, interviews, and participation are data that you can go back to, review, and consult.[1] Images are not intended to replace written notes, but when used in conjunction with them, they can be invaluable research data. Just as your written notes (regarding any particular social movement, healing ceremony, religious or secular celebration, or political conflict) may serve as a valuable resource for further analysis—that is, as data—the same is true of visual imagery.

Sociocultural dynamics that are particularly amenable to visual analysis include people, places, processes, performances, and practices. As is true with all research, the types of data you collect should be appropriate to the questions you are trying to answer. Behavioral observations, interviews, and surveys (among many other methods) only make sense *if* and *when* they help you understand something. It does not make sense, for instance, to try to determine what a poem means to someone by observing them or to describe a performance solely through interviews. In just the same way, different types of visual data are relevant to different types of research questions.

Let us take a political rally as an example. What do you want to know about it? If you want to analyze attendance (e.g., how many people were there, who attended, where different parties were located in the room), a still image, or series of images, will probably be best. With this you can go back and analyze your data—in this case your images—to get answers. If you are more interested in the tone of the exchanges and how people interact with one another, then video would be a better choice. The issue, then, is twofold: (1) What am I trying to understand? and (2) What will best enable me to explain my findings?

In Marion's work with elite ballroom competitors, for instance, still images facilitated understandings of body positioning, tone, and lines whereas video best facilitated understanding actual movement, musicality, and performance. It is no more "just taking pictures" or "getting some video" than it is "just taking some notes" when doing fieldwork. Without any idea about what you will be paying attention to or why, notes and images are all but useless. This is when thinking of images as data is most important. By choosing what to pay attention to and in what ways, you create useful information—not simply a haphazard collection of images.

So what types of questions ask for visual answers? Almost all observable phenomena lend themselves to visual questions and answers. For instance, from more pragmatic to more conceptual:

- What was the setting or location?
- What was there and how was it arranged?
- Who was there and what were they doing?
- How were they positioned and/or dressed?
- What were the relationships between the participants and things present?

As this list begins to suggest, visual methods and data "can be especially pertinent in investigating embodied experiences" (Pink 2006: 28), as well as physical settings. But why? In large part it is because "image speaks directly to the senses and emphasizes the human body and objectifications of culture and social aesthetics and social interaction, instead of ideas, meanings, and concepts" (Postma and Crawford 2006: 2).[2] Indeed, there is a longstanding tradition of such visual data—in the form of field sketches and diagrams—even before photographs and film. For example,

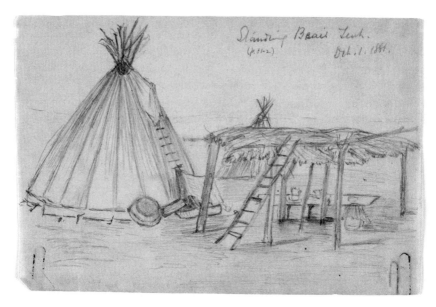

Figure 3.1 Fieldwork Sketch: Standing Bear's tent. October 1, 1881, as drawn by Alice C. Fletcher in her fieldwork diary, during her first fieldwork, and reproduced in her manuscript *Camping With the Sioux: Fieldwork Diary of Alice Cunningham Fletcher* (see http://www.nmnh.si.edu/naa/fletcher). Used by permission of the National Anthropological Archives, Smithsonian Institution (NAA INV 10000184). (Pencil and paper.)

during her first fieldwork in 1881, Alice C. Fletcher[3] produced many drawings as part of her field journals (such as the one seen here in Figure 3.1). Another example would be in 1892, when Smithsonian anthropologist James Moody lived on a Kiowa reservation and employed artists to make drawings for his field notes related to his ethnographic studies.[4]

So how do you go about getting good visual data? First, identify the needs of your specific project. For instance, just take a quick look at the case studies featured in each chapter in this book. Each study deals with different research projects that (a) use different visual data and (b) use visual data differently. In each case, however, there is a rationale for what was captured and how. One set of rationales comes from Karl Heider's filmic guidelines for framing whole people, whole bodies, whole interactions, and whole acts (see Heider 2006, Chapter 3). We do not, however, adhere to or see this as an orthodoxy. It is a conceptual starting point. It is important to craft images not only of the person/body/interaction/act in question, but to also get (a) broader shots that establish context and (b) more narrow shots that depict specific details.

While the balance between broad (whole) and narrow (specific), shots will depend on your own project's deliberately constructed questions and answers, having all three types of images is invaluable for documenting, analyzing, understanding, and explaining. More than providing distinct levels of information, having each type of image allows you—as a social scientist—to assess the relationships between these levels. Certainly Heider's suggested focus on the whole person/body/interaction/act makes sense in that, as social scientists, it is ultimately persons in whom we are interested. At the same time, part of understanding persons' actions involves wider perspectives. As Freeman points out, for instance, "environment can add a greater sense of the context and the space in which the activities depicted are taking place" (2009: 59). For this reason we advocate getting wider contextualizing shots if at all possible. At the same time, however, smaller actions and objects can be of central importance and can be missed without more narrowly focused images. Take a look at Figure 3.2. Each scale of image offers a different level of cultural understanding, but taken together they work synergistically, providing insight and understanding of how the different levels are interrelated with and influence each other.[5] So, again, getting all three scales of images is key.

Using Images to Illustrate, Explain, and Evoke

Hopefully you've started to think about images as data by this point in the book. But what type of data? Just as observations and interviews tell us different things, so do different kinds of images show us different kinds of things. More importantly, however, images communicate in a different way—they invoke understandings in a way that words alone cannot. Looking, seeing, and knowing are inextricably in-tertwined (Jay 1994, Jenks 1995), rooted in neurological and psychological links between visual perception, action, and emotion (Nijland 2006). It is along these lines that neuroaestheticist Semir Zeki has noted that "it is no longer possible to divide the process of seeing from that of understanding" (Nijland 2006: 38), and that Peter Biella (2009) invokes the real and powerful potential of ethnographic film to invoke intimacy and instigate social action.[6] If you have ever been moved by a picture or by a scene in a movie, you already know exactly what these scholars are talking about. It is the ability of images to evoke feelings that make visual data much more than simple illustrations. Images facilitate and catalyze understanding and insight.

Images show us many things simultaneously, which can be both powerful *and* problematic. Showing many things at once is a tremendous strength that reflects the all-at-once nature of lived experiences—a reality that is often impossible to com-municate through linear textual narratives. At the same time, whereas participants in real life situations typically know which elements and dynamics deserve the focus of their attention and which do not, this is unlikely to be true of those unfamiliar with the situation depicted. An image of a game with which you are unacquainted is unlikely to focus your attention on what would be central to a player of that game.

Figure 3.2 Context, Content, and Detail: This image shows a ballroom gown being produced by Doré Designs in Cape Coral, Florida, in August 2007. TOP LEFT: The first frame shows the dress itself—the primary focus of this sequence—on a mannequin. TOP RIGHT: The second frame shows the details of the individually hand-placed Swarovski crystals on this dress. BOTTOM: The third frame shows this process in action (on the left side of the frame) while also showing the bins of differently colored crystals (on the back wall) and the glue (front left) used to place each and every crystal. ©2007 Jonathan S. Marion. (Color originals.)

An acoustic record of a language you do not know will communicate very little in the way of denotative meaning. Similarly, imagery cannot be said to "speak for itself" *as data* any more than any other type of data. Part of using images as data thus involves the thought that goes into selecting and contextualizing images—whether as supplements to printed text, in video, or in multimedia applications.

As suggested elsewhere (Marion 2011: 4), key questions to ask are if it is acceptable to those whom it depicts (as discussed in Chapter 1) and if the image adds to what is being discussed. Thinking about the images, five key considerations include the following:

1. Identify topics amicable to visual depiction (as per this chapter).
2. Discard images that only duplicate the content of other images already in use.
3. Discard images that only illustrate rather than explain: if seeing the image does not add insight or understanding, discard it.
4. Juxtapose images where the comparison evokes greater understandings.
5. Integrate images and words (e.g., captioning, narration, etc.) to facilitate understanding.

While most of these topics are taken up in Chapter 10, On Using Images, and in the Conclusion to this text, it is important to start thinking about the type of data that images can provide—including the meanings and understandings they can facilitate and transmit.

Meaning and Understanding

Thinking of and treating images as data allows us to then analyze them both for understanding and for meaning—different levels of analysis. Think about friends who show you photos from their summer vacation. Generally speaking, you can probably understand who was there and what they were doing from the pictures. But what do those images *mean* to you? Probably not much. Indeed, you would probably be more interested in the pictures of landscapes and buildings than in those of people you do not know. Now, compare your viewing against someone who was there when the images were taken or someone who at least knows the people or places in question.

The *meaning* of an image depends on the stimulus value it has for someone. Here is another place where treating images as data can facilitate access to both levels of information, both the overt goings-on as well as their meanings, both the etic (outsiders'/objective) and emic (insiders'/subjective) perspectives. The obvious content (e.g., who was there, what they were doing) is accessible. It can be reviewed however many times necessary, facilitates systematic analysis (as seen in Anne Zeller's case study at the end of this chapter), and can be returned to and re-evaluated in the future (but see Chapter 8 on storing, organizing, and archiving).

At the same time, images can also be used to facilitate an understanding of meaning through elicitations—an underutilized and often invaluable ethnographic tool whereby research participants provide context and insight to the researcher.[7] Far from a complicated methodology, just think of looking at family pictures from years gone by and all the stories this can trigger from those who participated in the events represented in the images. This—in a nutshell—is what photo elicitation is all about. It is one of the ways of using images that we will return to in Chapter 10. Here, just recognize that as social scientists we need to (a) find ways to record field data and (b) direct outsiders' attention to appreciate insiders' understandings. Images provide powerful vessels for exactly such recordings and translations. Whether you create your own images (e.g., Zeller's case-study in this chapter) or work from existing imagery (Buckley 2001, 2005, Wulff 2007), treating images as data allows you to unpack cultural meanings below the surface.

WHAT'S IN AN IMAGE?

Anne Zeller—University of Waterloo, Canada

Images can provide a wealth of meanings, whether they're illustrations or primary data. The problem with using them as data is devising a way to extract comparable data from a set of images in such a way that the data collection can be replicated. My own research is focused on communication patterns in nonhuman primates. One major issue with this is that primates move very quickly and it is almost impossible to record exactly what they're doing during communicative episodes without recording the data and analyzing it at a much slower speed than it originally occurred. However, when faced with a mass of film or video data or even with a series of still pictures, the problem of how to turn the images into comparable data must be solved. In this case study, I am using still pictures to exemplify the methodology I have developed for analyzing film. It can work for still images as well and for visually recorded human nonverbal data.

These are pictures of four *Macaca sylvanus* (Barbary macaques). The top left and right images are of a mother and daughter. The bottom-left is an unrelated female and the bottom-right a mature male. They're all making a threat face. Yet you can see that they all seem to have differences in their expressions. What I did to analyze this material was to divide the face and upper body region into individual areas of movement (such as eyelids, eyebrows, and nostrils). and then with different types of movements. I came up with thirty-three components, such as eyebrows raised, eyebrows lowered, nostrils flare, mouth open, mouth compressed, and so forth. My research question was whether there were regularities in the use of components that correlated with social

Figure 3.3   Comparison of Four Threat Gestures in *Macaca sylvanus*:
Wilma (TOP LEFT), Rosemary and infant (TOP RIGHT), Barbary (BOTTOM LEFT), and
Ben (BOTTOM RIGHT). ©2012 Anne Zeller. (Color originals.)

factors such as age, sex, or kin relationship. The other possibilities were that each
animal had idiosyncratic uses of components or that component use was random.
The last two seemed unlikely since communication with others seems to require some
regularity in the formation of the gesture. My null hypothesis was that component use
was random.

When I had completed the recognition and listing of components, I discovered that
I had included a number that had not previously been recognized. These included
nostrils flare and upper lip stretch. I then sorted the film I had into segments which were
useable (clear and close enough to see the face in detail) and began to analyze it
frame by frame. If you just have still pictures they can also be analyzed this way. For
example, in the illustration the individual (W) in the top left is showing piloerection,

ears back, eyebrows lowered, eyes stare, nostrils flare, upper lip stretch, mouth open threat, mouth open wider right, no teeth show, mouth curved down, and body forward. When W is compared with the female in the top-right (R), you see piloerection, ears back, eyebrows lowered, eyes stare, nostrils flare, upper lip stretch, and mouth curved down. This is not identical to W but over a series of pictures there are more similarities between the related animals than between nonrelated ones. The female in the lower-left is showing mild piloerection, ears back, eyebrows raised, eyelid flicker (where you can see the white of the eyelid), upper lip stretch, and mouth closed. The male in the lower right is showing piloerection, ears forward, eyebrows raised, eyes staring, nostrils flare, upper lip stretch, and mouth open threat. You will notice that piloerection occurs in all of the animals and is one of the four components that occurred in over 90 percent of the threats and by all individuals, so I labeled these constant components. Other components occurred in all, or all but one threat expression in an individual animal, and these were the ones that I used to compare the groupings of the age, sex, and kin group. There were also some individually used components.

With this data I was able to conclude that facial threats in primates were not hardwired, and that they could probably recognize family relationships since the social grouping with the most similar component use was kin group. I was also able to conclude that the constant components were in the upper region of the face and the variable ones were around the mouth region, which indicated that different parts of the face provided different contributions to the message. I was also able to compare the component use in threats with that in friendly and fearful faces and recognize that these components were used in a variety of gestures (as are phonemes in human languages). In addition, I compared component use in three different species of macaques to assess how similar their gestures were. Very little of this would have been demonstrable if I had not had numbers that could be statistically analyzed, which was only possible because I had firm numbers of components to work with, rather than verbal descriptions of faces.

Summary

This chapter highlighted the use of images in asking and answering research questions. Beginning with the types of questions that can be addressed with visual data, we considered (a) how images illustrate, explain, and evoke understandings differently than text, and (b) how thinking of and treating images as data allows us to then analyze them for meaning and understanding. Building on the ethics of making and working with imagery (Chapter 1) and fundamental ideas of thinking visually (Chapter 2), this chapter's considerations of what it means to think about the image as data sets up the next section of this book, which deals with the actual making of images.

- *Beautiful Evidence* (Tufte 2006)
- *Researching Communications: A Practical Guide to Methods in Media and Cultural Analysis* (Deacon 2007)
- "All Photos Lie: Images as Data" (Goldstein 2007)
- "Do Photographs Tell the Truth?" (Becker 1986)
- "Questions of Process in Participant-generated Visual Methodologies" (Guillemin and Drew 2010)
- "The Visual Essay: Redefining Data, Presentation and Scientific Truth" (Simoni 1996)
- "The-Walk-in-the-City: A (No)ordinary Image: An Essay on Creative Technologies" (Antonaki 2008)

Section 2

MAKING IMAGES

4

CAMERAS IN SOCIAL SCIENCE RESEARCH

In this chapter you will learn about:

- The basic history of camera and image use in the social sciences
- How the purpose and use of images in social research has evolved
- Implications of the digital revolution for image making and social research

Overview of Cameras in Social Science Research

Not all social scientists want to produce images while conducting fieldwork. Perhaps images seem inapplicable to their interests or redundant to their observations. As with the eye, the camera does not see everything. Rather, it "sees" where it is directed, recording the light reflecting or emanating from a subject. Some people view such recording as objective, whereas others see it as subjective. In either case, photography—and cameras on the whole—have played a significant role in the production of social research.

Moving and still images have been used to great effect as field records, sites of cross-cultural interaction, sources for analysis, objects of study, and as visual and sensory systems to inspire further inquiry (Edwards 2011: 187). Yet cameras and images have fallen into and out of favor over time as both a method and analytical tool. Our stress, however, is the central role the camera can play in social science research—providing a virtually inexhaustible, inexpensive, and relatively unlimited means for making, sharing, and analyzing images. Even if you do not publish those images, images (moving and still) are a source of data for enhancing field notes, elicitations, and documenting aspects of research less amenable to textual notes or memory. Recognizing the ubiquity of images in the digital age, this chapter opens the door to important considerations of cameras themselves and their role in social science research.[1]

The purpose of this chapter is to outline how the camera has been used in social science research over time, and explain how thoughts about representation—that is, why and how to make and use images—in research has changed. For example,

100 years ago some researchers used images to document the "Other" as almost objective, scientific specimens by photographing indigenous people to indicate both biometric proportions, as well as adornments. We realize today that objectifying people in such a way is inappropriate, unnecessary, ethnocentric, and unethical. Scientific images of the past differ from contemporary ones both because the technology has drastically improved and our thinking about the role of research with people has progressed. The following discussion serves as a foundation upon which you can build your own opinion about the use of images in research, because knowing why and what has already been done engages you to consider why and how you may want to make images today.

Basic History

In the early nineteenth century, metals were the first medium for permanently capturing an image with a camera,[2] a process that required exposure to dangerous chemicals. Rather fragile glass plates followed metal in the 1850s, and were also dependent upon tricky chemistry and technical knowledge. After much experimentation and refinements, film came to the photographic process about thirty years later. Leaving the chemical process to popular labs, this was a revolutionizing technology allowing almost anyone to make images. Once still images were captured on film, it was not long before multiple still images were put together to make a motion picture, as the Lumière brothers did in 1895 (see Nichols 2010).

As noted in Chapter 2, social science researchers who were early adopters of photography included Franz Boas, who made hundreds of images (Jacknis 1984) and influenced the likes of Alfred Kroeber (see Figure 4.2), Margaret Mead, and Gregory Bateson. Their use of photography and film in their research on character formation in different cultures (the Balinese in particular) became seminal in the realm of visual anthropology.[3] Also of note is F. E. Williams,[4] an anthropologist with the Australian government in the Territory of Papua who hauled a box camera and tripod in order to make more than 2,000 images between 1920 and 1939 with glass plates and film of eighteen different groups of people scattered across the island. Within the same period researchers and explorers such as A. C. Haddon began filmmaking, followed by the likes of Felix-Louis Regnault and Baldwin Spencer, known for their interest in accurately depicting the lives of Others (El Guindi 2004).

Realism and Objectivity: The Science Behind the Camera

At the beginning of the twentieth century photography and filmmaking were regularly employed by researchers—with Western academics leaving for the field and taking cameras with them to capture moments of "natural" life, which would

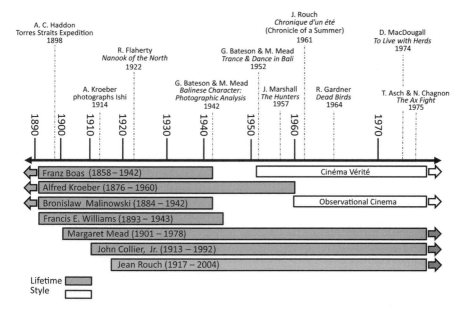

Figure 4.1 Chapter Timeline: This timeline depicts some of the key contributions (and contributors) to visual research and ethnography mentioned in this chapter. This diagram is not intended as a comprehensive history of the subdiscipline or related fields. Rather, it helps illustrate the content of this chapter while also serving as an example of how visual representations can be used to augment textual materials.

Figure 4.2 Kroeber Photographing Ishi: Alfred Kroeber photographing Ishi, photographed by Saxton Pope in 1914. Photo courtesy of the Hearst Museum of Anthropology (15–5835). (Black-and-white original.)

later serve to supplement their written descriptions of the culture. Cameras were thought to provide accuracy never known before, and were considered to be completely objective tools that both (a) removed the researcher from the subject and (b) enhanced the image of the Other for the reader. In the right hands, as Mead explained, the ethnographer recognized the culturally significant moments that could be "captured" for study (Mead 1975/2003: 7). Ethnographers strove to collect broad and comprehensive information on their subject matter and images dramatically enabled that goal.

By mid-century, ethnographers in the Americas, Europe, and Japan were involved with making films to preserve images of the peoples they encountered, with as little bias from the filmmaker as possible. These efforts involved recording human movement using eye-level cameras on tripods. However, as cameras became easier to handhold, filmmakers like Jean Rouch started to follow their subjects around, creating a *cinéma vérité* (Rouch and Feld 2003), or truthful cinema (i.e., lifelike). This genre was much less objective in perspective and quite dependent upon what researchers found relevant to their work. Still, the literature remains replete with the call to use the appropriate method to answer the specific question, meaning that cameras (moving or still) were only to be used when visual data helped to answer the research question at hand or to supplement the ethnographic data and subsequent analysis.

Along these same lines, universities were formalizing the study of visual anthropology with the intent of building archives of films representing peoples of the world which would serve as data for later study, discussion, and ultimately, knowledge. While these histories are well documented,[5] the gist of the enterprise illustrates an embrace of image as data (as discussed in Chapter 3) and a move towards the scientific, both in terms of production and analysis. Some projects were stricter than others concerning who could be involved and how film could be shot. For example, guidelines were established that required filming be done by persons with significant anthropological training, that scripts and logs be kept to authenticate the subject matter's worthiness, and the end product be as representative as possible (eschewing cinematic liberties, dramatic angles, and a soundtrack) (El Guindi 2004: 31–2).

Prioritizing the Interpreted Image

Similar debates within photography argue for the product of the camera as objective reality, on the one hand, and as artistic expression on the other. Indeed, these conversations continue within the social sciences to this day (Harper 1988, Pink 2009) and continue to be argued within various disciplines.[6] Today researchers also frequently use handheld cameras in their work and the images they produce tend to reflect their own ways of seeing (i.e., what they understand to be happening from their expert perspectives). Because of the many meanings that images may evoke, academic disciplines and texts often marginalize the role of the image in research as being too difficult to control—that is, as destabilizing scientific premises of objectivity and replicability. It was along these lines that, from the 1970s through the 2000s, (a) visual anthropology was marginalized (by most) within the larger discipline and (b) relegated to making classroom films to teach anthropological concepts, rather than being seen as a medium through which new knowledge and critiques could be created (Pink 2009: 13, Chaplin 1994: 16).

Now known as the "theoretical turn," by the 1980s the social sciences were moving away from (but not abandoning) strict scientific inquiry and turning towards a fuller understanding of reflexivity, subjectivity, and mediation as part of the research process. Visual approaches were affected by this turn too, with ethnographic filmmakers and photographers recognizing their inherently subjective positioning at all stages in the production, use, and analysis of images. As in text-based ethnography, where the author is the instrument through which all data is captured and analyzed, so too is the case when holding a camera. The researcher's presence influences both what is captured and how. Even when the camera is not directed toward exploring specific research questions, it still affects how people respond to the researcher.[7] The reflexive trend, with its emphasis on the subjective role of the researcher—in this case using a camera—helped shift the focus of ethnographic imagery from capturing "the data" to describing the mundane and the extraordinary alike.

None of this is to say that the arts (photography) and creative process were absent from earlier ethnographic fieldwork and production. Among others, the work of Robert Gardner (e.g., *Dead Birds*, 1963) and David MacDougal (e.g., *Doon School Chronicles*, 2000) exemplify the creative use of cinematographic techniques, such as unique angles, long pans, and quick edits to draw the viewer into the film and make meaning by incorporating symbolism and abstractions (e.g., constructing dream or hallucinogenic trip sequences) and highlighting tensions within filmmaking. **Observational Cinema** blended the methods of scientific observation with the storytelling of documentary filmmaking. It was originally an experimental approach located along the edge of the theoretical turn, where filmmakers placed themselves in the films, affecting the representational endeavor. However, with the turn, visual ethnography intensified its draw on artistic photography and filmmaking while becoming one of many visual techniques for social science research (e.g., Young 1975/2003, MacDougal 1975/2003, 2006, Grimshaw and Ravetz 2005).

To be clear, some products of visual research fueled the theoretical turn itself. With terms like "subjectivity" and "colonialism" now commonplace social science terminology, the disciplinary gaze fell upon anthropology's past to reflect its role in defining the Other, much of which was accomplished through the publication of images. Boas, Williams, Evans-Pritchard, and many others—whose earlier images served to illustrate an "objective" account of culture—became fodder for criticism and discussion, and in some ways served to justify the interpretive turn. Their use of images came to serve as the indelible line between (a) the scientific use of images and (b) the interpretive recognition of self in image-making that continues to demarcate positions within visual research. In other words, the scientific images of the past were scrutinized for their ethnocentrisms and colonial undertones, propelling criticism on the use of images in research and what they mean for social science in the first place (see Lutz and Collins 1991, 1993, Hastrup 1992).

Small discrepancies between the use of photography in sociology and anthropology were founded upon the analysis rather than the subjects' specifics—although until recently these disciplines were typically split along a Western/non-Western divide. Unlike the anthropologists mentioned above, sociologists were more likely to analyze historical photos that their subjects may have taken of their families, jobs, or affiliated institutions (whereas few of the non-Western peoples had cameras of their own). As digital cameras have become more and more commonplace (including those in cell phones, tablets, and other devices), it has become possible for people around the world to make images and record video that anthropologists, sociologists, and other social scientists find worthy of analysis, thus blurring the distinctive line—if not erasing it altogether—between ethnographic and popular intent.

Technology's Role

While some scholars have preferred to trace the theoretical directions of visual anthropology through text-based ethnography, technology consistently provides new mediums for social inquiry and human engagement. Unfortunately, many who embraced visual technologies at their inception did so to support the idea that non-Western cultures were less evolved. As Mead, Malinowski, and Rivers demonstrated, however, there were other uses for images than defending one's cultural superiority, including investigating people on their own terms. Even so, Mead (1975/2003) admonished her anthropological colleagues for developing a science dependent upon words rather than images. In that vein, John Collier, Jr. (1967/1986, 1997) argued that visual anthropology could show the "organic cultural whole" by documenting the culture through images—the only way to represent the empirical to other scholars (Biella 2001: 55). The logic was that since the hard sciences valued photography as representing facts, using film could legitimate anthropologists' data (Collier 1997). Paul Hockings (1975/2003), on the other hand, insisted that visual anthropologists employ all media available in order to educate people about themselves.

At any rate and at its best, there seems to have been a continuous call from within the social sciences to use the available technology to extend the study of the human condition. Any such study thus depends upon what is technically possible at any given time. Riding the digital revolution out of the twentieth century presents a more expansive media horizon than heretofore imagined—but that is also what ethnographers thought about the first still and video cameras. Ultimately, however, technology facilitates two things:

1. It allows us to do what we already do better.
2. It creates an opportunity to do new things.

The still camera and audio recording equipment thus became permanent components of the ethnographic tool kit because they were seen as practical for capturing cultural data and being scientific. The movie camera was not seen as essential, however, because early moving images did not have synchronized audio and few academics accepted it as evidence. It also did not help that the equipment was big, awkward, heavy, unreliable, and somewhat dangerous. Furthermore, it required significant expertise to work, and it was already a daunting task for an anthropologist to do both film and audio simultaneously, let alone also conduct an interview at the same time.[8]

As physical film developed—both with greater light sensitivity and color— several other innovations were also underway. First and foremost, cameras were becoming smaller and lighter, and could now be removed from tripods and moved indoors. Up until this point, researchers had to ask their subjects to move outside to film an activity that took place in low light.[9] With early technological innovations and improvements, however, filmmakers and ethnographers could show the regular settings of indoor and lower light events, more intimate scenes, and also follow their subjects on the move. Jean Rouch perfected this *verité* style, permanently changing the genre and role of the camera in research. Then, with the advent of synchronous sound, as used in the MacDougals' *To Live with Herds* (1974), the viewer no longer had to be told what people were saying—they could hear it for themselves; giving voice to indigenous people (albeit often with subtitles of selective translation).

Arguably today's technological innovations mean that we no longer conceive of, or conduct, visual ethnography as was done half a century ago. As digital mediums have evolved—becoming smaller, lighter, less expensive, and easier to use— the power to create and manage images is no longer determined by the few who possess heavy, stationary cameras, but rather now resides in ubiquitous handheld electronic devices. Not only can still and moving images be made with the same camera (including synchronized sound), the images may now be viewed around the world without ever being reproduced on paper or film. The opportunities created for using digital equipment in the field raise questions (as discussed in Chapter 1) regarding how we conduct our research, whose images are made (including how, and under what circumstances), and with whom these images are ultimately shared. Thanks to the Internet we can communicate with people in villages and cities all over the world, introducing ourselves in remote places before arriving and continuing our relationships after leaving. Certainly, sharing images with the research participants increases buy-in through an understanding of the work you are doing and the research you are conducting. The immediacy of digital media (versus the latency experienced with film) can greatly enhance participant interest and trust.

As digital equipment has become ever-more commonplace (for example, the visual features integrated into cell phones) many researchers no longer think about doing visual research—rather, cameras have become part of the common ethnographic toolkit. This means that the use and analysis of images are no longer relegated to the margins of social sciences like anthropology and sociology, but have become central to the endeavor.[10] The fact that research participants can (and often do) continue to make videos, which they upload and share for themselves after the researcher departs, illustrates the multi-faceted issues involved in conducting research of any sort these days.[11] Untangling the ethical components of visual research requires the researcher to consider factors never before addressed, as we see in Chapter 1. At the same time, it opens up opportunities for working with and using photography, video, and multimedia as part of our ethnographic toolkit as displayed in Karen Nakamura's case study below and as described in the following chapters.

THE DYSPROSODY OF IMAGES

Karen Nakamura—Yale University, United States

In the 1970s, photographer W. Eugene Smith took a series of evocative, heartbreaking photographs of children severely disabled by mercury poisoning in the town of Minamata in western Japan. The international attention that Smith brought to this small community helped them eventually win damages from the company and acceptance of responsibility by the government.

If a picture is worth a thousand words, how much control do photographers have over the words that their viewers evoke on looking at their images? In Smith's case, the deformed bodies of the children affected by the environmental pollution—as well as the solution—was a narrative easily understood by his audience.

As a visual anthropologist of Japan, I also take photographs and make films about people with disabilities. In 2004, I started blogging about disability protests in Japan on my blog. I took photographs of the activists (Figure 4.3, top and left) that indicated the passion that they brought to the protests. Even though many had quite severe

Figure 4.3   Dysprosodic Images?: TOP and LEFT: Japanese disability protests. RIGHT: Tsutomu with his guitar. ©2005 Karen Nakamura. (Black-and-white originals.)

physical, intellectual, or psychiatric disabilities, they braved the cold winter weather to bring their claims to the Japanese government.

As I blogged about the protests, I realized that many of my readers reacted strongly to the visceral quality of the visual images, but often skipped over the accompanying text. Because their bodies were visibly disabled, readers imagined pathos and helplessness.

But this was exactly the opposite of what the protesters themselves wanted to convey. At the time of the protests, Japanese people with disabilities had attained an enviable array of independent living services and programs. The government was threatening to roll these back and move them towards an American system of pitiful benefits and a substandard quality of life. The protesters wanted to make sure that their gains weren't being rolled back; they were afraid of losing their independence.

The problem with photographs is that if the subject material is too alien, viewers may entirely misread the nature and content of the material. This is what I call the dysprosody of images and it is a fundamental problem that all ethnographic photographers struggle with.

Viewers need cultural context in order to understand photographs; the photographs themselves cannot convey all of this and can often be fundamentally misunderstood. Anthropologists attempt to capture the richness of other people's lives. Ethnographic photographers are challenged to find mechanisms to make readers understand the stories behind the images to help see the world through different lenses and not their own distorted visions of the Other. Accompanying text and captions can provide insight, although these are easily skipped. Other ways of staging photographs and audio or textual material together—such as streamed photo essays used by Magnum photographers—or other forced multimodal linearity can help with the issue of dysprosody.

Is film one solution? The opposite situation to the photographs of the disability protests occurred when I started to explore psychiatric disabilities such as schizophrenia and other severe mental illnesses. Because mental illnesses generally cause invisible disabilities, still images do a poor job of conveying important aspects of these peoples' lived experiences. Looking at my friend, Tsutomu, with his guitar (Figure 4.3, right), it is difficult to understand what is going on in the interiority of his mind.

Frustrated with my experience with the dysprosody of still images, I shifted to ethnographic filmmaking where I was able to make my subjects speak in their own words to the viewers. In my film, *Bethel* (2007), Tsutomu comes to life and tells us directly what he experienced as a patient in psychiatric hospitals and we also come to understand how he has negotiated with the symptoms of his illness over time.

Summary

This chapter provided a brief history of camera use in social science research. First, we looked at early research that used photography in the field, and the intent to gather images that were considered accurate and real slices of life from the field. Early equipment was quite cumbersome, however, drawing significant attention to the photographer and required significant expertise to use effectively. Within the past few decades, cameras, photography, and filmmaking have become far more accessible (and much less obtrusive), opening up new possibilities in fieldwork as new technologies allow different types of images to be created. This chapter concluded by briefly noting some implications of the widespread availability and use of digital equipment; images can immediately be shared with a subject on the one hand, and almost as quickly transmitted around the globe on the other—with the potential for influencing subjects' willingness, understandings, concerns, and investments in the research process and endeavor.

- *An Anthropologist in Papua: The Photography of F. E. Williams, 1922–39* (Young and Clark 2002)
- *Anthropology and Photography: 1860–1920* (Edwards 1992)
- *Photography and Anthropology* (Pinney 2011)
- *Principles of Visual Anthropology* (Hockings 1975/2003), especially:
    - "Ethnographic Film and History" (Lajoux 1975/2003)
    - "Ethnographic Photography in Anthropological Research" (Scherer 1975/2003)
- *Working Images: Visual Research and Representation in Ethnography* (Pink, Kürti, and Afonso 2004)

5

PHOTOGRAPHY

In this chapter you will learn about:

- The advantages and disadvantages of still imagery
- The role of intent in creating photographic images, including the relationships between researcher, subject, and audience
- Basic photography and composition concepts that will enable you to better (1) analyze and understand the photographs you view and (2) think about and create the images you want in your own work

There is no one way to do research, and there is never just one way that you should use imagery in your research. Rather, it is crucial to think about (a) what types of imagery will serve you best, and (b) in what ways. It makes no sense, for instance, to decide that you want to produce pictures, video, or multimedia without understanding the advantages and disadvantages of each. Chapters 6 and 7 will consider video and multimedia respectively. We will start in this chapter with still images, as these sometimes stand on their own but are also often included with text, in videos, and as part of mixed media.

Advantages and Disadvantages of Still Imagery

What is photography good for and what is it not good for? While there is more than one way to answer this question, it all ultimately comes down to the fact that what still photography does is freeze an image of what was happening in front of the camera at a specific point in time. This is both photography's strength and its weakness. In Marion's work on competitive ballroom dance, for instance, dancers' posture is better displayed in a still image, whereas their movement style is better shown via video. The numbers of people at a ritual or the appearance of a specific object are far easier to assess from a photograph, whereas how the ritual was performed may be better depicted in video. What people were thinking is probably not best captured in a photo (although facial expressions may be very revealing of feelings) and an image will do nothing to capture sounds and smells. But what

Figure 5.1 Ch'alla in Juli, Perú: November 2003: David Onofre and his family sit on the floor of their house during a *misa blanca* offering ritual. We met the diviner (*yatiri*), who appears in the lower right corner, in a small village near Lake Titicaca and invited him to David's family's home in Juli to perform a cleansing ceremony. This photo serves as a strong image for photo-elicitation at a later date because one could discuss the various family members present and the space in which the ritual occurred, as well as the paraphernalia (coca leaves, llama fat, wine, etc.) used during the ceremony. Everyone is smoking in order to purify the space before the ritual continues. ©2003 Jerome Crowder. (Color original.)

people were doing, how they were dressed, and their appearance? Here (as with architecture, geography, and such) photographs are exceptional. They allow viewers to study multiple details simultaneously, serially, at length, and either in isolation or in relation to each other in a way that linear media (including video) do not permit (see Figure 5.1).

Photographic Intent

Initial questions for using images include: Why are you taking pictures? What role do they play in your project overall? Here is where your intent as the researcher

and photographer matters. In short, what work do you expect your images to do? Are they meant to be memory triggers somewhere down the line, either for you or some of your research participants? Are they meant to document specific people, places, or events? Are they meant to give an overall impression of a certain setting or situation? Or do you even know how you want to use them yet? All of these are viable, but each (a) needs its own kind of image, and (b) involves different relationships between researcher, subject, and audience. Here, Figure 5.2 illustrates the significance of photographic intent in crafting your images.

Images that you reference for your own recollection are different from images that are shared with the community, both of which differ from the images that you use to present your research. Taking good ethnographic pictures depends on social and cultural sensitivity, and may be contingent upon personal rapport (as per Figure 1.1) and careful negotiation. In such cases photography can serve as a powerful ethnographic passport to social and cultural understanding, especially to communities that value such images (Marion 2010). In all cases, the types of images you take (and how you then use them) are inextricable from how they were made, what they are meant to show, how they show, and to whom they are visible. Thinking about and understanding what types of images you want, and to what ends, is what allows the previsioning (noted in Chapter 2), which is the ethnographically-informed understanding of what image will best show what you want to show.

Key Photography and Camera Concepts

As we have been discussing, what you want from your images matters. In the end, that is up to you and should be guided by ethical and ethnographic considerations. Knowing what type of images you want, however, is different from being able to create them. While we think it is great that more and more people want to incorporate images in their ethnographic toolkit, we also recognize that most social science

Figure 5.2 Photographic Intent: All four of these images were taken at the 2007 British Open Dancesport Championships (perhaps most widely known as the Blackpool Dancesport Festival) in Blackpool, England. All four were shot from the first balcony level, but with very different intent: the general setting and busy floor of morning-time practice, including (relatively) informal outfits (TOP LEFT); the congested floor of early rounds of the competition (TOP RIGHT); the spectacle of the final rounds of this prestigious competition, from the more open floor to the spotlights to the formally attired spectators (BOTTOM LEFT); and the focus of all of these other elements, the best dancing by the best couples in the world, in this case, Blackpool and World Professional Ballroom Finalists, Victor Fung and Ana Mikhed (BOTTOM RIGHT). ©2007 Jonathan S. Marion. (Color originals.)

programs offer little in the way of technical training. The purpose of this chapter is thus to help you better (1) analyze and understand the photographs you view and (2) think about and create the images you want in your own work.

Exposure

Simply stated, the **exposure** or **exposure value** (EV) of an image is the amount of light received by the camera sensor (or film). While there really is no such thing as a good or bad exposure, in common use images that are too light or too dark are said to be "bad" exposures, whereas an image that is correctly exposed is said to be "good." Unlike the typical on-and-off light switch in your home, however, your camera controls how much light reaches the sensor in three interrelated ways: shutter speed, aperture, and sensitivity.

Shutter speed refers to how long the sensor is exposed to light, and is typically expressed in fractions of seconds. For example, a shutter speed setting of 1/60s exposes the sensor to light for 1/60th of a second (long exposures are expressed in seconds, e.g., 4s). While some recent cameras have more options, for the most part each successive shutter speed roughly halves the exposure time (e.g., 1/30s, 1/60s, 1/125s, 1/250s). Faster exposure times (i.e., a faster shutter speed) captures action better—for instance, you typically need shutter speeds of 1/250s (or less) to "freeze" human action—but this also allows in less light since each halving of the shutter speed also halves the amount of light getting through.

Where shutter speed controls how *long* (duration) light is getting through to the camera sensor, it is the **aperture** (also known as the iris)—the adjustable opening in a camera lens—that determines how *much* light reaches the sensor (per unit time). Aperture settings are rated in f-stops, and are written as f/4 or F4 or 1:4 ("4" is being used here for illustrative purposes only). What is key to understand is that because f-stops designate fractions of focal length, higher numbers (e.g., f/11 versus f/8) represent a smaller aperture opening (see Figure 5.3). As such, successive aperture settings *halve* the amount of light reaching the sensor.

Think of the aperture setting as an adjustable-width water pipe. When the pipe is open to a quarter of its maximum width it would only allowing though half as much water compared to being set to half its maximum width. To continue the water pipe analogy, camera lenses literally function as light pipes, and the maximum aperture of a lens is what is referred to as **lens speed**.[1] Because lenses with a large maximum aperture (rated as a small f-stop) can allow just as much light through in a shorter period of time (i.e., at higher shutter speeds) these are called fast lenses.[2]

The third variable that factors into overall exposure value is the sensor's sensitivity to light, described by its **ISO** setting. ISO is not an acronym, but rather stands for the International Organization for Standardization, a nongovernmental organization dedicated to establishing shared standards for business, government,

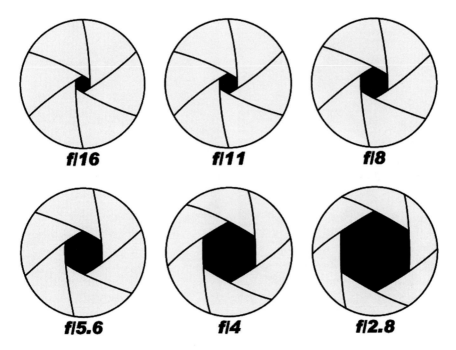

Figure 5.3 Apertures.

and society (see www.iso.org). The higher the ISO rating, the greater the sensitivity to light along a linear progression; for example, a 400 ISO setting is twice as sensitive as 200 ISO in exactly the same way as 400 miles per hour is twice as fast as 200 miles per hour. But what happens when there are bumps in a road? Yes, you get there sooner when you are driving faster, but you also feel each bump and bit of debris that much more as well. In essence, driving faster increases the impact of the bumps just as it increases the distance covered per unit time. Higher ISO settings work in just this way as well—they amplify the sensor's sensitivity to *all* input, allowing for images using less light, but also creating less sharp, more pixelated, and less well-defined images. It is the amplified "bumps" of images shot at higher ISO settings that photographers refer to as the "noise."

So why does any of this matter? Because now that you realize that you can achieve the same exposure value in different ways, you can better control the types of images you take. One of the ways this can show up is in controlling the **depth of field** (DOF) of your image, which is the zone of acceptable sharpness both in front of and behind the main focus point. Do you want the foreground or background somewhat blurry (to help keep attention on the subject), or do these need to be in sharp focus (perhaps to provide important contextual information)? While every lens and every situation is different, here are four basic rules:

Figure 5.4 Depth of Field: These images show a competition ballroom dress being decorated by Doré Designs in Cape Coral, Florida. Using a very shallow depth of field, focused on the foreground, one image (LEFT) draws attention to the design and detail on the hem of the dress being decorated. The other image (RIGHT), in contrast, uses wider depth of field, focused on the mid-ground, to highlight the person and the process of placing rhinestones on individual dots of dress glue. As these images illustrate, DOF can be used to deliberately direct attention to specific elements. ©2009 Jonathan S. Marion. (Color originals.)

1. Larger aperture = shallower DOF
2. Smaller aperture = greater DOF
3. Closer to subject = shallower DOF
4. Farther from subject = greater DOF

Because you now understand the inverse relationship between aperture and shutter speed, you can make the adjustments you need to in order to control the DOF. Figure 5.4 provides an example of how this all fits together.

Before turning to actual image composition, it is important to differentiate between **image resolution**—defined by number of pixels in an image—and image quality. If you think of a pixel as a small bucket for light, it should be clear that pixel quality (which depends on many variables) makes a difference, and is not a simple matter of more pixels being better. How big is the sensor for the camera in your phone for instance? The number of megapixels may be high, but each pixel will be considerably smaller than in a larger digital camera. In essence, there may be more buckets for light, but each bucket is much smaller. Rather than getting bogged down worrying about having a camera with more resolution, focus on the quality of the images produced, especially in whatever output (e.g., online, in print) you intend to use them.

Another pitfall to beware of concerns optical zoom versus digital zoom. **Optical zoom** refers to a lens' capacity to use its optics (i.e., to bend light) in order to make a subject appear closer to the camera. There really is no such thing as digital zoom. The camera may look like it is zooming in further, but in fact it is digitally enlarging a smaller portion of the sensor frame. In other words, once the optical capacity of the lens has been reached, digital zoom is pulling adjacent pixels apart and extrapolating what should go between them. This reduces image quality to be sure, but remember our discussion of images as data in Chapter 3? Well, using digital zoom is letting your camera's processor fill in what it thinks the data should be! Would you want to do the equivalent with your written field notes? Probably not. So worry about the optical zoom available on your camera (or video camera), and avoid using digital zoom unless there is absolutely no other option whatsoever—and, if you have used digital zoom, always keep that in mind when going back to that digitally constructed image and treat any such data accordingly.

Other important factors to consider are the memory media and image formats you will be using. The physically small but ever-larger digital capacity memory cards in use today are a real advantage of digital photography. Compared to film, far more images can be recorded, with far less time spent switching rolls, with on-the-fly frame-to-frame ISO adjustments, and with the immediate feedback possible from reviewing the images on the camera itself. Because of ongoing developments and advancements, we do not want to bypass any detailed discussion of the various digital camera storage media. In most cases your choice of media will depend on your camera, and for most purposes the different storage media function in similar ways. CompactFlash (CF) is the format used in most high-end cameras and is the most stable overall, but SecureDigital (SD), SecureDigital High Capacity (SDHC), xD Picture Cards (developed by Olympus and Fuji), and Memory Sticks (developed by Sony) are all perfectly viable.

The only storage media to avoid are MicroDrives. These small hard drives look and fit like CF cards, but because of their many moving parts are far less stable (and drain more battery power) than any of the other media types. Just like you would not write field notes on paper that might disintegrate, do not take field images using MicroDrives! MicroDrives aside, the two important variables in selecting your storage media are (1) its storage capacity—how much digital data it can hold—and (2) its write speed—how quickly images write from the camera's processor to the card and how fast the card then downloads images to your computer. Unless you will be taking a lot of fast-moving action images (with multiple frames per second) or you will be taking hundreds or even thousands of images at a time before downloading, the write speed of most cards should be sufficient.[3]

As far as storage capacity, the number of gigabytes (GB) you will want depends on several variables. In the first place, what is your camera sensor's resolution? Higher sensor resolution means that you will get fewer images (because the size of the files is respectively larger). Also realize that it can be much better to have more cards with less data on each in case of loss, theft, damage, or failure. In any case, though, the number of images you can get on your card depends on image format. While there are many image formats in use today, the three most important ones for our purposes are RAW,[4] JPEG, and TIFF.

As the name suggests, RAW files are exactly that—all of the data. While more basic cameras only shoot JPEG files, more and more cameras allow you to shoot in RAW (or sometimes in both simultaneously). The files are much larger (meaning fewer images will fit on your storage media), and these images need specialized software to view (such as the software that comes with your digital camera, Adobe Lightroom or Photoshop, or ACDSee Pro). For both of these reasons many people prefer to shoot in JPEG format. As visual researchers, however, we cannot overstate how important we feel it is to shoot in RAW whenever possible. To understand why, you have to realize why JPEG files are so much smaller than RAW files. While RAW files record all the data at every point in the image, JPEG files are based on algorithms. In essence, if there are multiple black areas, green areas, or red areas, only the actual data for the first such area is recorded, and the compression algorithm then records additional areas as being the same as the first area where that color appears in the image. Viewing a RAW file is thus viewing a record of all the data, whereas viewing a JPEG involves looking at what a camera's image processor considered to be "like" data.

This is not to discount the utility of the JPEG format when making the most of limited storage capacity or when it will be important to be able to show images directly on someone else's computer or television. What is worth noting is that JPEG is not a lossless format, so data are lost when this format is used. This is where TIFF files come into play. TIFF files are very large and lack some of the post-processing versatility of RAW files, but share the JPEG format's ability to be viewed without specialized image editing software. TIFF files can be compressed with minimal or no loss in quality.

Image Composition

Carrying over from 35mm SLR cameras, full-frame DSLR[5] cameras show roughly the same field of view as the human eye using a 50mm lens, making 50mm a "normal" lens. Lenses that show a broader field of view are considered wide-angle lenses, and lenses that provide a narrower field of view are considered telephoto lenses. Figure 3.2 provides an example of the difference between these perspectives. What we most want to stress here, however, is that the wide, normal, and telephoto images *are different*; that is, they show different things, even if they are all of the same subject matter and are "pictures of the same thing." This highlights how little sense it makes to think of any image as good (or bad) except in relation to specific intentions or criteria.

Another important variable concerns the source and location of light in your image. There are probably more photography books written about lighting than any other subject. This makes sense when you realize that recording reflected light *is* photography. Rather than try to summarize this vast topic, we suggest a quick exercise: Pay attention to the light outside at dawn, midday, and dusk. The light will be coming from different directions, from different heights on the horizon, and with different colors. Now what about on a clear day, an overcast day, and a cloudy day? Next, pay attention indoors. Notice that things look different by window light versus candlelight, and under incandescent versus fluorescent lighting. The point here is that there is no way to photograph "just what was there," since the same thing can look quite different at different times and with different light sources.[6] Figure 2.6 illustrated this indoors, but we want to stress that flash can be advantageous outdoors as well, as seen in Figure 5.5. Again you need to ask yourself, which image best helps you show what you want (and why)?

A final idea we want to introduce regarding composition concerns subject placement. First and foremost, do not center the focus circle in your viewfinder on your subject's head! This leads to the most generic images possible and wastes half the frame with space above your subject. More to the point, think about people you talk to and interact with: your focus is not equally above and below their face, so why would you produce an image with this type of focus? Instead, and whether dealing with people, objects, or landscapes, we suggest using the **rule of thirds**, a strategy whereby an imaginary tic-tac-toe grid is used to help create a more visually interesting and compelling image. This strategy helps move you away from horizon lines that essentially split the image into a top and bottom half, and place key elements at points of visual interest (i.e., the intersections)[7] as seen in Figure 5.6.

Terence Wright's case study in this chapter provides a strong example of using photography as part of the research process itself. In addition, the resources listed at the end of the chapter point the way to learning more about photography. For the moment, however, you should have a much better idea of the advantages and disadvantages of still imagery, a better understanding of the basic technical issues and terminology, and some ideas about composition. Based on these ideas, how can you look at, understand, and analyze still images differently from before? More importantly, what ideas does this give you for crafting your own images?

Figure 5.5 Daytime Flash Outdoors: Crowder made this image while riding in a tricycle taxi in Puno, Perú. Although there is plenty of light, the flash fills in the shadows cast on the driver's face and upper torso by the canopy, balancing the exposure. This image also provides another example of the previsioning discussed in Chapter 2, as Crowder had seen this image in his head for months and then worked to find the appropriate driver willing to be photographed. ©2005 Jerome Crowder. (Color originals.)

Figure 5.6 Rule of Thirds: Notice the difference between the cropped version of this woman walking by and the full version of the same image. The bricks and beams of the wall in the full image suggest the imagined grid of the rule of thirds, and connote a fuller sense of atmosphere and movement than the cropped version of the image seen on the right. This image also provides another example of provisioning (Chapter 2) in that Crowder, having previously noticed how the late afternoon light fell on this wall in El Alto, returned to the location and waited for someone to walk by. Although walking in the opposite direction than anticipated, Crowder framed the image placing the Bolivian woman in the leftmost third of the image to imply movement. ©2000 Jerome Crowder. (Color originals.)

IRISH FRONT GARDENS

Terence Wright—University of Ulster, Northern Ireland

In Ireland, people rarely inhabit or use the front garden for any real practical purpose (other than car parking). Instead it often becomes a site of individual expression, adorned with ornaments that may represent the householders' personal interests or display links to a romantic or historic past. In Northern Ireland, garden displays can be overtly political, featuring loyalist or nationalist insignia, or they can perpetuate a vernacular style linked to Irish wayside shrines, grottoes, or "fairy" trees. The garden displays can reflect a fantasy world where myth and romance feature alongside nostalgia for an idealized past.

My visual research project takes an anthropological focus on this aspect of Irish domestic architecture. As a case study in this book, it represents some initial thoughts and work-in-progress concerning the ways I have used photography to compare and contrast garden displays. The photographs have been taken in a frontal style, whereby the back of the camera has been positioned parallel to the front of the building. This has the result of reducing the degree of perspective recession in the photograph, so that the house forms a flat backdrop to the garden display. This approach aims for a type of *realist* image insofar as the photograph reproduces a miniature facsimile of the façade of the building (Wright 2004: 40–1). At the same time, the framing of the houses aims to be all-inclusive: the image doesn't focus on any individual aspect of the garden; rather it allows viewers to discover for themselves or to be directed to specific elements pertinent to the study.

In one of the photographs, the semi-detached construction of the houses facilitates a comparison within one picture. From what is a standard 1930s house design in the United Kingdom and Ireland, inhabitants have embellished the building to their own tastes: styles of fencing, *faux* shutters, different selections of windows and doors, and so forth. The display of a traditional cartwheel in the right-hand garden is juxtaposed by the choice of a Chelsea Football Club insignia on the left-hand side. One house is partly hidden by shrubbery, in stark contrast to the manicured topiary horse and rider of the other. And while one has a pair of neglected plastic Regency-style plastic

Figure 5.7 Irish Gardens: TOP: This picture would normally be printed at a size of 20 x16 inches, enabling viewers to see detailed information within the photograph. BOTTOM: Here three details from the larger image are shown to help illustrate and support some of the information in the text. ©2004 Terence Wright. (Color originals.)

urns either side of the doorway, the other has a pair of cannons to greet the visitor. Some items such as the horse have been uniquely fashioned, others (such as the urns and statues) purchased from ornamental garden suppliers. In fact, one could continue creating a list of comparisons between the two dwellings that have been constructed as mirror images of each other. Indeed the hard and fast dividing line between the two properties (created by the respective owners) reinforces the bilateral or reflective symmetry of the photograph.

Camera Equipment: Flash, Batteries, and Storage

Space permitting, we would have an entire chapter related to flash photography. Remember, the most basic mechanism of photography *is* recording the light reflected back to the camera sensor—nothing more and nothing less. As such, flash can determine if you get a shot or not, especially if you are in a dark setting or your subject is heavily backlit (i.e., the light is silhouetting your subject from behind). The benefit of flash is seen in Figure 2.6, where it opens up what the viewer can see of a high-contrast indoor setting; and in Figure 5.4, where it balances out bright sunlight. Likewise, almost all of Marion's ballroom competition images depend on flash, both to help freeze action, but even more so as a necessity in often dimmed ballrooms with very mixed lighting (including hot spots, dark zones, colored gels, and spotlights). Especially if you do not have professional-level fast lenses, then, flash will be the only way to get many images; so be sure to (a) research the types of flash available for your camera, and (b) recognize this as a crucial investment.

Finally, before you start any project, we want to remind you to think about the batteries your camera and flash will need, and how you will be carrying your equipment. Can your camera use AA batteries or does it use a camera-specific rechargeable battery? How many batteries do you have? How long will these last you? How and when will you have opportunities to replace or recharge these in the field? Remember, even the best digital cameras are no better than paperweights without power. Your camera (and flash) are also useless if you do not have them with you or if they break. Here is where having a camera bag can make all the difference in the world. Again, think about where you are going and what will be most important to you—there are camera bags for every situation! Some are larger and some smaller, some protect your equipment better, some are less conspicuous, some offer better weather protection, and some will hold a laptop or tablet computer. If you get the chance, try fitting your equipment into a bag before you decide if it is the one for you. No matter what, once you have found a bag, figure out a system for packing it *and stick with it*—this will help you keep track of all of your equipment in the field.

Summary

Focusing on what still images do, and how they do it, this chapter began by assessing the comparative advantages and disadvantages of different types of visual media (with video and multimedia being addressed in the next two chapters). Starting with the role of intent in creating photographic images, we explored the triadic relationship between researcher, subject, and audience (first introduced in Chapter 1). Next, highlighting key considerations involved in making and analyzing images, we focused on photography as a tool for capturing behavior as seen by the user. We then introduced basic photography and composition concepts (e.g., framing, shutter speed, and ISO settings), allowing you, the reader, (1) to better analyze and understand the photographs you view and (2) to start thinking about and creating the images that fit your work.

Further Readings and Resources

- *Photography* (Bull 2010)
- *The Photography Handbook,* Media Practices Series, 2nd edition (Wright 2004) is especially good regarding visual literacy
- *The Photographer's Eye: Composition and Design for Better Digital Photos* (Freeman 2007)

6

VIDEO

with Elizabeth Cartwright

In this chapter you will learn about:

- The advantages and disadvantages of using video for research
- The role of intent in creating video
- Production pitfalls to avoid
- How to evaluate the visual importance of your research

Choosing whether to use video or still photos (or both) depends on your resources, equipment, and the ultimate goals of your work. Chapter 5 outlines some of the basic differences between still and moving pictures; in this chapter we continue to explore that issue in more depth. We briefly outline basic video shooting techniques for specific situations, such as interviews or action sequences, and then address the pitfalls to be avoided when making videos. Our intent is to clarify basic techniques of video production and to encourage the reader to continue pursuing the art and science of good ethnographic videography.

Advantages and Disadvantages of Video in Research

The temptation with video is to shoot too much. This cannot be overstated. The digital capabilities of good quality handheld and prosumer video cameras give the videographer huge amounts of shooting time. Gone are the constraints of a few reels of film (or tape). In the old days, because production costs were prohibitive, a great deal more time had to be spent thinking about what one was going to film before starting to record. While the ability to shoot for long periods of time can be handy, and a few things will be captured that otherwise would have been missed, often those perfect seconds of outstanding video remain buried among hours and hours of lousy footage.

So, why use video at all in your research? Video allows us a small window into lived realities that no other medium can provide. It shows process and captures actions and words as they naturally occur in the flow of experience. This provides us with a multidimensional way of capturing the essence of whatever we are studying. By simultaneously capturing verbal and nonverbal acts, ethnographic video provides access to multiple levels of behavioral data. Ethnographers continue to write down what is being said by those they work with, thus creating a textual record of what is a lived social exchange. With video you can watch a storyteller's face, see how expressions change, and watch body gestures. This opens up a whole new array of analytical spaces for conducting and representing ethnographic research.[1]

Intent

In light of these possibilities, the questions you must ask yourself when considering the use of video in a research project are: (a) what is visually interesting or compelling about the research I want to conduct, (b) does moving imagery help record this better than still imagery, and (c) if so, how? In answering these questions, you must decide if something fundamental to your project cannot be captured by any other means—in other words, will video analysis provide insight that is unattainable any other way? Poor answers to these question include, "it would be cool to make a film about it" or "I won't know exactly what I'm trying to say until I begin shooting."

Thinking about your audience is key to answering the "why visual" question and, as we discuss below, may determine the equipment you wish to employ. Depending upon the research topic, video data may be for analysis only. The footage you shoot will have a limited audience (yourself, your research team) and its main purpose may be (a) to review multiple things happening at once, or (b) to verify other observations you have already made. Ethical issues (see Chapter 1) may also preclude your footage from ever being shown publically.

Or, if you plan to make a video to accompany research (perhaps for an advocacy piece or documentary), you will have specific audiences in mind that will affect how you frame and construct the inherent message of the work. Be careful when considering a video component to research, as a video production may easily supersede the research itself. That is, your focus can easily be distracted from research to filmmaking, particularly if your funders or a community group expect a video product that promotes their position. Before recording even one minute of footage, take time to understand the expectations of *all* involved. This will serve everyone better in the end.

Beginners often assume that a video presentation will be a popular means for sharing their research. Such a plan can very quickly become fraught with politics and issues beyond your control, discouraging any action at all. You must clearly share your intent for the video/film with everyone involved and keep that goal in mind during all phases of production. Written consents[2] to use images need to be obtained and signed copies should be kept in your files. If you cannot sufficiently answer the "why visual?" and "why video?" questions, stop. Do not consider video until these answers are clear to you and clear and acceptable to those with whom you are working.

On the other hand, video can enhance and help refine research questions, and possibly even create completely new ones. If you determine that video will help you answer a research question, there is a strong probability that it will also enable you to develop new ones. Cartwright's case study demonstrates how the use of video did not yield what they expected to find, but instead created a new way of approaching teaching techniques.

LEARNING TO USE A NEW MEDICAL TECHNOLOGY—EXCERPTS FROM A VIDEO-BASED STUDY

Elizabeth Cartwright—Idaho State University, United States

We used video-based data in order to understand the process of legitimate peripheral participation (Lave and Wenger 1991) among flight crew members of a rescue helicopter as they learned to use a new ventilator system.[3] Our methods were designed to focus on visually capturing the process of learning a new, complex piece of medical technology and then systematically analyzing the resulting video data. While systematic text analysis has become a standard in qualitative research, the systematic analysis of actions has received less attention. Thus, our research focused on the analysis of the nonverbal actions that occurred as team members were introduced to and became more familiar with a new piece of medical equipment.

During the training, the ventilator was attached to a mannequin and an instructor interacted with the nurse or paramedic in a one-on-one teaching interaction. The teaching event was videotaped from beginning to end resulting in approximately thirty minutes of visual and audio data for each instructor-learner dyad. Seven instructor-learner dyads with four different instructors were included in the study. One of the most important results from the study was that regardless of teaching style employed, the students all significantly increased their interactions with the new ventilator over the course of the training session. Often, students in this kind of learning environment will complain that they didn't get enough time to really work on the machine. By using video-based research methods, we were able to show exactly how much time students were given during different segments of the instruction, thus allowing for a more fine-grained understanding of this particular learning event.

Just because you have determined that video will help you answer a research question does not mean that it will be easy to obtain useful data, despite how easy technology has made it to gather footage. We write this not to scare you, but to encourage you to think through exactly *how* you plan to capture the footage you need in order to do your work more effectively. The following topics represent key components of video-making: stability, composition, audio, lighting, and practice.

Nothing is more distracting than shaky video. Your viewers expect a clean, stable shot, and in order to achieve this, you must stabilize your camera in some fashion. Image stabilization technologies (built into the camera or lenses) cannot fully counterbalance jitters from shooting hand-held video. If you are going to spend the money on a video camera, you need to take stabilization seriously. If appropriate (e.g., for interviews, fixed or slow moving subjects), placing your camera on a solid tripod achieves this in a simple and straightforward manner. Because a tripod can limit your mobility, however, it is not perfect for every situation. Handheld shooting allows for on-the-move filming (as per Bishop's case study in Chapter 2), and can also be used as an intended effect.[4] Even when shooting hand-held video, you can learn to use your body as a tripod (see Figure 6.1), including panning by rotating your trunk (i.e., never your arms). The bottom line is (1) make sure your shots are steady and (2) always consider how you will do this, whether using your body, tripod, or other stabilizing device.

Once you have your camera steadied and ready to go, it is time to think about composing your shot. Use all the same principles that you would to compose a really good still image (i.e., the *mise-en-scène*, as per Chapter 2). Think through subject placement, depth of field, and watch out for distracting background elements. If you are setting up an interview, place the subject off-center, remove any extraneous objects from the interview frame, and do not shoot with a window or a mirror in the background if at all possible. Move your subject until they are nicely framed in a way that allows the viewer to focus on the person who is talking, not on something popping out of the background. Also, as noted in Chapter 2, the human eye naturally moves to the point of greatest contrast on the screen, so take care with your composition. Video, unlike a still photograph, has that added component of motion that you can use to your advantage while framing your shot. Think how the repetitive motion of a swing or a teeter-totter can be used to draw the attention to the

---

70

Figure 6.1 Stabilization and Sound: Videographer Michael Brims (Visualization Program Director, TLC2 at the University of Houston) is seen here stabilizing his video rig by holding his elbows close to his body, and his feet spread wide—effectively creating a tripod with his arms and torso—during a handheld shot in Fallbrook, California. He follows the couple by pivoting at his waist, not turning his arms, to keep the shot steady and smooth. The two people walking past him are wearing wireless lavalier microphones to capture their discussion. The high tones of their voices are balanced with the mounted shotgun microphone, which picks up the lower frequencies. All audio is fed into a multichannel field mixer (in his shoulder bag) and then into the camera, which he monitors with headphones. ©2012 Jerome Crowder. (Color original.)

part of the frame that you want to highlight. Be aware, motion draws attention. As such, it can easily distract more than it adds.[5]

B-roll

To make strong and compelling video, you need more than talking heads and action shots: you need footage that (1) helps you transition between scenes and (2) keeps the viewer from getting bored of watching people talk. This is where B-roll comes into play. **B-roll** refers to the supplemental footage that you can use to add context and meaning to a sequence, to transition between scenes, or to eliminate unwanted content.[6] Both as you are planning and shooting, think about the ancillary shots (e.g., establishing shots, public activities, events) that could help you tell a story. For example, what footage could you later weave into your video to help illustrate whatever your interviewee is discussing? Never underestimate the usefulness of having B-roll, as it significantly enhances your ability to flesh out whatever topic you cover.

Audio

Complementing steady video is quality audio. Even if you have the most beautiful, steady shot of people conversing, if the synchronized audio is noisy, scratchy, or inaudible, you will lose your audience. Humans are accustomed to sound being a part of their viewing experience. Even old silent film actors had lines they had to mouth because audiences needed to read their lips to pay attention. Video production is no different, and if compromised by poor audio your work becomes almost worthless to your viewer. Arguably, sound quality is more significant than video quality. For instance, think of all the video clips posted on YouTube and Vimeo, or those recorded on mobile phones. You probably accept this suboptimal video without much thought, but quickly get irritated by garbled, poor quality audio.

So, when investing in your camera and tripod, you should also consider purchasing complimentary microphones. We are not advocating the most expensive available, but we do encourage you to research appropriate microphones (or mics) for the kind of shooting you plan to do—especially as there are several different types, each with its own kind of pick up pattern, application, and transducer (see Table 6.1 and Figure 6.2).[7] The most common microphones are omnidirectional (picking up from all directions) and directional (picking up from specific directions). Do not assume that your camera's onboard (built-in) microphone is sufficient for decent video production: it is not. As we have stated numerous times now, ensure the best possible audio for your video or do not bother to do it at all. This makes headphones essential gear for producing good audio, as they allow you (or someone else on the crew) to monitor the level of the audio being recorded on the soundtrack of your video.[8] In-ear or over-ear styles may matter, but not as much as the fact that you use something to listen to the audio your microphones are capturing!

Paul Henley (2007) underscores the importance of environmental sounds and how they constitute a soundscape for ethnographic filmmakers. When well employed, such audio thickens the film's descriptions, enhances the viewer's experience, and intensifies the film's effects. In essence, he argues that contemporary digital filmmakers should consider the aural as much as the visual in all aspects of production as this will greatly increase the quality and complexity of their films. Steven Feld's (1990, 2004) explorations of acoustemology (one's sonic way of knowing or understanding the world) describe the importance of sound in everyday life and how the acoustic complements the visual experience of film. It helps us understand why we expect audio when we watch film. In considering our aural and visual perceptions of the world, what makes sound so powerful is that we do not recognize the ways that it affects us (Erlmann 2004, Thom 2003).

Table 6.1   Microphones Frequently used in Videography.

Type	Common pick-up (polar) pattern	Application	Transducer
handheld	unidirectional/cardioid	lectures	dynamic
shotgun	highly directional	limited distance	condenser
boundary	omnidirectional/variable	focus groups	condenser
lavalier	directional	interviews	electret

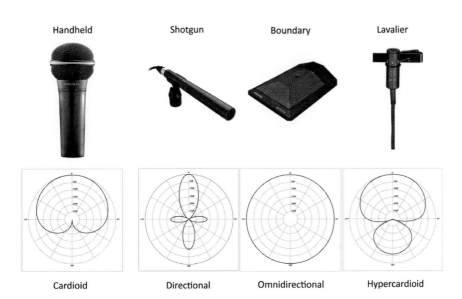

Figure 6.2   Microphones and Pick-up Patterns: Some of the more common microphones you can use in your filming, and their respective pick-up patterns.

Figures 6.3 and 6.4 show the attention to audio we have been advocating (also see Figure 6.1). Notice, for instance, a dedicated soundperson on each team who is using different types of external microphones and monitoring the audio pick up through headphones. Steps that can be taken not to compromise the quality of the audio being produced can be seen in Figure 6.3 in the use of a sound baffle (or Zeppelin) on the shotgun microphone to prevent picking up any wind noise. Figure 6.4 shows another important audio consideration: the use of nonverbal signals between the camera and sound persons during filming.

Lighting

Having even lighting will help your subjects appear lifelike and real. No amount of postproduction can help you resolve overexposed, underexposed, or spotty footage.

Figure 6.3   Sound Matters: Joanna Casey shoots video from a ladder while sound-person Kimbra Smith raises the boom microphone with Zeppelin (sound baffle) attached to capture the sounds of the craftsman working on a boat. National Science Foundation (NSF)-sponsored Short Course in Research Methods 2008, North Carolina Maritime Museum, Beaufort. ©2008 Jerome Crowder. (Color original.)

Unlike shooting RAW and color digital photographs, which allow you to manipulate the exposure value in post-production, digital video (and most certainly film and analog video) require nearly perfect exposure at the time of recording. Tweaking digital video exposure values can be tedious and inconsistent in the end, so we advise you to consider the quality of your lighting sources before shooting. Since an office or other interior space can be congested with different types of light (e.g. incandescent, fluorescent, natural light coming through windows), continuous light kits (e.g., halogen or LED panels) are available that will even-out the lighting on the face of someone being interviewed. Even outside shots can be improved with artificial light

Figure 6.4 Nonverbal Signaling: Cameraman Jonathan Marion communicates with soundperson Courtney Carothers while shooting a boat builder at the North Carolina Maritime Museum speaking with patrons. The patrons' faces have been blurred to protect their identity because we (a) take our ethical obligations seriously (as per Chapter 1) and (b) do not have consent forms from these persons. National Science Foundation (NSF)-sponsored Short Course in Research Methods 2009, North Carolina Maritime Museum, Beaufort. ©2009 Jerome Crowder. (Color original.)

since clouds, trees, buildings, and other shadow-casting objects can wreak havoc with natural lighting (on faces in particular). Besides lights themselves, less expensive options like reflector cards (gold, silver, white) can be used to bounce light back onto your subjects more evenly.

Like the digital sensor in your still camera, the video camera's sensor must also be set to recognize what white looks like. Whether you are outside during sunny or cloudy conditions or inside using incandescent or fluorescent bulbs, each cast a different spectrum of light. You may notice such differences when moving from one setting to another (such as stepping outside at sunset and noticing how orange things seem to be), but most of the time you do not see these differences because your brain adjusts for what your eyes are "seeing." Where your brain constantly re-adjusts, this is not true for your camera, so you need to define white for the camera before you begin shooting. In other words, depending upon the type of light you are shooting in, white can vary greatly so defining white under your particular circumstances is fundamental to natural looking results. Most cameras can do this automatically using an AWB (automatic white balance) setting, but (a) you need to do this each and every time you go to shoot and with every change of your setting; and (b) be sure to check your manuals in advance (and practice) in order to know exactly how to make these adjustments on your camera.

Practice

No technology substitutes for practice. As with still cameras, you must be familiar with your equipment so that when you need to use it, you can. Fumbling around with your equipment can be annoying for your subjects or can cause you to completely miss the shot. We suggest that you read the owner's manuals and keep them with your equipment for easy reference. Even more importantly, practice using your equipment; get to know its idiosyncrasies so you are prepared for and can address them appropriately. Subject your friends to mock interviews or shoot family gatherings to become familiar with your camera and different situations. For example, practice walking steadily with the camera to figure out what works best for you and your team, and shoot in low light and bright light situations to figure out how to adjust your equipment to compensate. Whatever you do before you go live will yield exponential gains in video quality (Figure 6.5).

An example of what can go wrong without sufficient practice with your equipment comes from a group of Marion's visual anthropology students in 2009. Running late, the group of three students each signed out professional quality video cameras from the campus equipment desk, including a variety of external microphones. Arriving at their filming location (for a project on roller derby), the students plugged the microphones into their cameras and spent the next three hours filming training and practice bouts of the local roller derby team and interviewing several team members. Not having sufficiently familiarized themselves with these cameras, however, the students did not realize that the jacks for the external microphones were not "live" (i.e., active), and the students got no sound from three hours of observational and interview footage using three different cameras.

As this case should make abundantly clear, practice with your equipment as much as possible before you ever use it in the field. Likewise, pay attention and check yourself as you go. Note, for instance, that if even one of these students had remembered to use headphones they would have noticed that they were having a problem with sound. Also, realize that there are ethical implications to this error as well. It can be quite problematic to have nothing to show your participants after they have given you access to their lives, as well as their time and effort (e.g.,

Figure 6.5 Practice First: These three professors (Fuji Lozada, Maris Gillette, Scot Lacy) attending the Short Course in Research Methods Video Analysis course practice single camera interviewing before going into town. Here, for instance, they try using a pad of large white paper as an improvised reflector to help light the subject's face. ©2008 Jerome Crowder. (Color original.)

for an interview). Similarly, what type of social capital will it cost you to redo your filming—if you even can?[9]

In our experience, we have found that a routine for setting up your equipment (tripod, camera, microphone, lights) in a set order (which is logical to you) effectively serves as a checklist so you can catch problems before they arise. After-the-shoot routines will also keep you ready to go the next time, such as recharging your batteries and placing them in the same pocket of your bag, or formatting your digital cards and keeping them in a card holder that is always placed in the same pocket of your camera bag. Be aware and be prepared. All too often forgetting to recharge batteries or download digital cards can ruin an interview or one-time shot opportunity. Just like writing field notes following every interview, making a habit of dealing with your digital data and the equipment each time helps keep yourself organized and prepared for your next shoot.

Evaluating Your Video Intentions and Objectives

Thanks to relatively sophisticated handheld video technology you can begin implementing and evaluating your answer to the "why visual" question without depleting your research budget. Small high-definition video cameras (e.g., FLIP, Kodak Playsport, GoPro) make it easy to introduce video capture into your research with simple-to-use and easy-to-access video devices, and then allow you to evaluate the recording immediately.[10] We recommend making a number of short one- to three-minute clips of what you find visually compelling or appealing about your research. Experiment with your composition. In reviewing the shorts, consider whether or not you actually captured what you intended to. If possible, upload the shorts into a video editing application (there are many free ones out there) and splice the scenes together to make a very short piece—ideally no longer than five to seven minutes. Share this with friends, colleagues, and the subject(s) of your video and ask for their feedback.

At this point, it is up to you to determine whether to pursue a more sophisticated video production. In any case, however, at least you will have tested the utility of video for your research question and can then develop new ideas about how to approach your question visually if you were not successful the first time. If nothing else, stand-alone video snapshots can serve as informative means for describing behaviors (e.g., repairing boats, making food, street dancing, healing rituals) that enhance your written descriptions or elicit further discussion with your participants. Positive responses may indicate the need for a more sophisticated production, requiring an evaluation of appropriate equipment and personnel to realize the final product.

Jennifer Wolowic's case study illustrates how video became a tool for research analysis, as well as an incentive for participants of the First Nations youth she works with in Canada.

FOR OUR STREET FAMILY

Jennifer Wolowic—University of British Columbia, Canada

For Our Street Family (Wolowic 2007) is a film about a group of First Nations youth who attended a teen drop-in center in Prince Rupert, British Columbia. The project began as a photographic group self-portrait when the dozens of teens at the center took pictures of one another. Hundreds of images of play, love, and pain were created, but these pictures only gave glimpses into the youths' strong peer-support network.

In between snapping camera shutters, the youth called their friends their "street family" and referred to each other in kin terms. Best friends held the title of auntie or sister. Friends who advised others became parents, regardless of age or genetic relationships. The street family solidified friendships and strengthened peer support for young people facing challenges at school and with biological family.

Video provided a way to explore the story of the street family. With video camera in hand, I asked several of the teens to draw their family tree. As I recorded, the youth

Figure 6.6 Planet Youth: On a sunny summer afternoon when their teen center is closed, eighteen youth gather at the park next to City Hall. Often called a gang by people walking by, these youth find comfort and laughter hanging out with their friends. Photo by Chrystel Cooper. (Color original.)

debated for over thirty minutes and mapped out forty names and relationships. This scene was dissected and became a major structural component of the film. Footage of youths mapping their family was interlaced with images of the teen center and five interviews about their experiences with foster care, teen alcoholism, abuse, and racism. These stories help explain why their street family exists.

For young people who often described feeling invisible, sharing their experiences on film became a way to be seen and feel heard. However, video required a strong relationship between participants and myself before they felt comfortable in front of the camera. Video also destroys all protection of anonymity as people become directly associated with what they do and say on screen. When piecing together the film, immense care had to be taken to respect participants and avoid sensationalizing their experiences so that they would not become victims of backlash.

Sounds of laughter, visions of smiles, intense tragedy, and recorded encounters affectively engage audiences to learn from youths who are negotiating ambivalent identities, the pain of stereotypes, and their vitally important peers. For a group usually labeled or ignored and so often parented by bureaucracy, video offered a medium to share their stories.

Further Educating Yourself

There are vast resources available online, and throughout many cities across North America and in Europe, of which you should avail yourself. Do not underestimate the effectiveness of one-day or weekend workshops sponsored by continuing education programs, professional organizations, and art centers. Enrolling in a one-day or multi-week course will dramatically improve your (pre and post) video production skills, which will in turn enable you to better evaluate your answer to the "why visual," "why video," and "how" questions. You do not need to enroll in specifically ethnographic filmmaking courses to learn the fundamentals of video production for social science research. Instead, share your ideas with the instructors and learn about how to achieve your visual research goals. We have each significantly benefitted from taking many different types of courses from places like the Salt Institute, Pittsburgh Filmmakers, Houston Center for Photography, and Maine Media Workshops, to name a few.

Summary

In this chapter we stressed the need to consider the visual aspects of your research and how they translate to video, remembering that not all research easily does. Once you have decided that important aspects of your work are visual, you need to ask yourself how video helps you make your research point. When preparing to shoot, think about what you need (previsualize) and do not shoot too much just because you can. Consider your participants' assumptions about video: Are they willing to work with you and be on camera, and do they understand their role in the video? What are your audiences' expectations? Consider how your participants and audiences may have very different expectations for what to do with the video once completed. Equipment considerations include a camera, appropriate microphone, sufficient recording media, and appropriate lighting (even if just in the form of an improvised reflector). Based on production pitfalls to avoid, this chapter suggested several keys to getting your video to work for you, including keeping your camera stable, composing your shots, ensuring good-quality audio and lighting, and practicing regularly with your camera before shooting when it really matters.

Further Readings and Resources

- *Beyond the Visual: Sound and Image in Ethnographic and Documentary Film* (Iverson and Simonsen 2010)

- *Cross-Cultural Filmmaking: A Handbook for Making Documentary and Ethnographic Films and Videos* (Barbash and Taylor 1997)
- *Reflecting Visual Ethnography: Using the Camera in Anthropological Research* (Postma and Crawford 2006)
- *Handbook of Participatory Video* (Milne et al. 2012)

7

MULTIMEDIA

In this chapter you will learn about:

- The evolving role of multimedia in research and presentation
- How to assess the strengths and weaknesses of multimedia
- Effective means for implementing multimedia in your research

Multimedia, as the term itself implies, uses more than one type of media to present its content. Each type of media—audio, video, image, and text—provides different dimensions of information, and combining them creates multidimensional content. Rather than just providing multiple layers of content, when done well multimedia approaches work synergistically to create something more: a symphonic whole. For instance, because humans listen while watching (see Chapter 6), good audio makes good video (i.e., video without audio is less interesting because it is less normal). In other words, the combination of media enhances researchers' effectiveness in conveying information and meaning.[1]

The History of Multimedia

The first workshops and classrooms designated as "multimedia" meant being equipped with large screens to use with projectors, a VHS tape player with stereo sound, and an amplified speaker podium. Bringing these technologies together allowed for more effective communication. Audiences now experienced different types of analog media at one time that engaged multiple senses simultaneously, and thereby enhanced the overall experience. These rooms were used for slide shows, films, and videos that were presented linearly from start to finish. The digital revolution and the advent of the web gave rise to nonlinear media, that is, media that are not necessarily produced or watched from beginning to end as texts are expected to be read. Unlike older analog slide shows or films that had to be fast-forwarded, for example, webpage hyperlinks allow viewers to immediately move from digital chunk to digital chunk of information, and to do so in unique combinations and sequences. The term "web" thus describes the multiple links that connect topics and issues within multimedia documents.

The second generation of the World Wide Web, Web 2.0, moved the Internet experience to the interactive level (see, for example, Wesch 2007). No longer was the viewer/user moving through static webpages, but instead was engaging with the material directly—leaving comments, forwarding content to others, sometimes editing the text itself, and even uploading one's own material. In similar ways, social networking connects multiple users, creating meaning through their relationships as they navigate a never-ending, always evolving terrain on the Internet. The dissemination of visual research has started to take advantage of the online multimedia environment, and is likely to continue along lines that have not yet evolved or been recognized when this book is printed. The key question, however, is what can be gained by linking different media together in various configurations and relationships?[2] We next discuss some of the more popular means of doing this.

PowerPoint Presentations

For visual researchers, multimedia is an opportunity to combine various types (or dimensions) of data together into one product like a webpage. Researchers most commonly use PowerPoint slide shows for academic (or business) presentations, as these are not difficult to develop with basic backgrounds, text, and images. There are, however, differences between simple and complex PowerPoint presentations (El Guindi 2004) with the former only utilizing text and images (which all too often are simply read to the audience—yawn). More complex slide shows integrate animations, video, overlays, and other media, while depending on the presenter to speak alongside the slides. The presenter is responsible for bridging the material for the viewer, recounting narratives, and serving as an interface conduit between audience and material.

It is not our purpose here to teach you to build effective PowerPoint presentations (although please see Chapter 10 for related points regarding using visuals). Instead, we focus on PowerPoint as an elementary form of multimedia that can be (a) quite effective when used appropriately or (b) disastrous when misused. Unlike physical slide shows (using slide carousels), PowerPoint presentations can be easily modified: images and text can be rearranged and edited, animations and audio used as augmentation, and videos or links embedded. While this versatility and adaptability can be very useful, the different features available need to be used judiciously. It is all too easy to muddle your message and undercut the overall effectiveness of

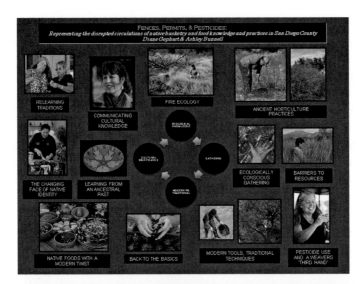

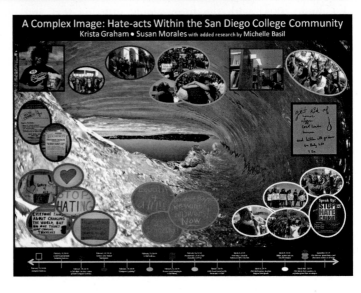

your presentation with purposeless—and therefore distracting—animations (e.g., flying text, special effect screen fades) or backgrounds (e.g., rainbows, sunbursts, garishly mismatched colors).

The fundamental principle of constructing PowerPoint presentations is the same as with all presentation strategies: Only use the images, text, or video that enhance the communication of your message. You must therefore keep in mind the nature of your audience and the conventions with which they will be most familiar. For example, while academic or scholarly presentations may require references and citations along with theoretical discussion, these would likely be quite inappropriate (distracting, boring, puzzling) for a public lecture, such as to a Rotary Club, that should have more images, less text, and perhaps address community service. Such an audience should not be distracted during the body of the presentation with references in small print that can be put on a final slide.

Posters

Perhaps the "lowest tech" and oldest form of multimedia is the poster, which is a highly effective and widely underappreciated means for presenting research findings. Nowadays a single PowerPoint slide may be sized and printed to very large dimensions to display text and images. As with slide shows, good posters require interaction between the presenter and the audience, so refrain from using too much text. Posters are not papers. Posters are best thought of as a research calling card; it should help you engage with your audience and allow you to speak to your project. A poster (just like a PowerPoint slide show) should augment your spoken presentation, not replace it—it shouldn't be designed so that your audience can read it while you stand there. Rather, it should present a series of key talking points—using text, images, and their relative configurations[3]—that can be expanded on and discussed by the presenter (see Figure 7.1).

Figure 7.1   Posters: MIDDLE: Four of Marion's students—Diane Gephart, Ashley Bunnell, Susan Morales, and Krista Graham—are shown presenting independent research projects as part of the Society for Visual Anthropology's Invited Poster Session, "Visualizing Circulations and Circulating Visualizations," at the 2010 American Anthropological Association (AAA) Annual Meeting in New Orleans, Louisiana. TOP: The image shows the poster by Gephart and Bunnell, "Fences, Permits, and Pesticides: Representing the Disrupted Circulations of Native Basketry and Food Knowledge in San Diego County." BOTTOM: In their work, "A Complex Image: Hate-Acts Within the San Diego College Community," Graham and Morales (with research by Michelle Basil) illustrate how posters can be used to present an overall picture with embedded cues for discussion. We also want to acknowledge the ethical issues—as per Chapter 1—involved in using a photograph that includes some of those attending the poster session (i.e., the non-presenters discussing the posters). Using this picture was not done without consideration, but only after assessing (1) the public venue, (2) the entirely voluntary attendance, and (3) the lack of any question or concern voiced regarding the prominent camera (e.g., note the flash reflection next to Morales's head) used to take this picture. ©2010 Jonathan S. Marion. (Color originals.)

In the future, professional meetings may provide flat-screen televisions or digital projectors for interactive posters. (There is no doubt that business conferences will be doing this.) Although unconventional at the moment, we have seen researchers take small digital projectors to poster displays. An already available and effective means for conveying your work to interested parties is to include your poster as an Adobe PDF file on personal or research websites. A more recent poster-related medium is the glog (graphics blog), an online collage of text, images, and video. These are simple to construct and are an excellent means for engaging students, but we have not yet seen these used in academic scholarship. The potential is there, however, and it is certainly a form that deserves careful consideration and further development.

Hypermedia

Since their inception, nonlinear productions have proven to be an attractive media for researchers because of the multiplex information they provide for users. When combined together, text, image, video, and sound create a multifaceted description of the research project that includes new levels of meaning realized between the media themselves. In other words, the different media complement each other in one production. While some media prescribe how such media are interlinked and presented, hyperlinks allow users to quickly move *within* an application—accessing the parts of the material in which they are interested, without having to scroll through the materials in a predetermined order. Also unlike conventional text, hyperlinks not only connect concepts, but also incorporate and involve users' choices and voices to construct more nuanced understandings of the material at hand. Usually provided in a CD or DVD format, hypermedia texts typically in-clude high-resolution images, along with detailed information—including primary sources, notes, letters, transcripts, and annotations—to provide users with a unique experience, all without congesting the flow of the project because users can focus on and explore what interests them most (see, for example, Figure 7.3 in this chapter's case study).

Whereas PowerPoint presentations maintain a linear structure, hypermedia does not. As such, hypermedia are significantly more complex to build and re-quire planning about how various nodes of information fit together, including how the multiple media interact with each other in different configurations. We want to stress this point: For a user to productively navigate through webs of hy-perlinked materials, the data must be well structured and organized. It requires the builder to think through the relationships between the constituent chunks of digital content.

When building image-based hypermedia projects, consider what you want your audience to know about the images, such as the images' content and context, how they were made, and how they contribute to answering your research questions. What else might users want to know? What questions might they have coming to your materials from their own backgrounds, agendas, and interests? We recognize that no project can be all things to all people (and that even trying to is a doomed enterprise), but it is crucial for visual researchers to consider how hypermedia move us beyond print materials by allowing for a far more inclusive presentation of our research. In print, we can provide notes, jottings, technical details, and reflections. With hypermedia we can go further and include sound (recordings of the people we work with), short video clips, and other layers of information and associations not possible with text alone.[4]

Particularly noteworthy hypermedia projects include those by Peter Biella and Carroll Blue. In *Yanomamo Interactive*, Biella (1997) revisits the well-known ethnographic film *The Ax Fight* by Timothy Asch and Napoleon Chagnon, allowing users to "instantly move to 26 significant moments in the film, view a slow motion version of the film with narration, and view an analysis of the film with genealogical charts" (Biella et al. 1997). Also as part of this CD-ROM-enabled experience, users can read text descriptions, view analysis, and research individuals through photos and genealogical relationships—all of which connect fundamental anthropological principles with specific cultural elements and thereby significantly enhance the value of the original film. Of course, multimedia CD/DVD-ROM discs require a computer and are, in essence, off-line websites.

Filmmaker Carroll Parrott Blue's award winning interactive multimedia production, *The Dawn at My Back: Memoir of a Black Texas Upbringing* (2003), showcases several features that make it worthy of note for social science researchers. Blue chooses to present an autobiographical narrative as book, DVD-ROM, and website to enable "direct interaction through an exchange of roles between author and reader," unlike the linear book in which everyone is presented with the same format and sequence of information (Blue 2004: 993). The book contains three parallel stories of a mother, a daughter, and a society dealing with the impact of racism in segregated Houston, Texas. The nonlinear DVD interface, however, provides users with hyperlinks—through the representation of a traditional quilt—to explore numerous photographs, letters, historical documents, poems, and journals, along with art, film, and original music and lyrics to better understand how she and others like her experienced Black life in the pre-civil rights South. Among the included media are documentary-style interviews with elderly Black Houston witnesses complimented by scripted, dramatic recreations by professional actors. Blue encourages the reader to then visit the website and enter into a dialogue with her by writing his or her own personal story—effectively reconfiguring the roles of story/author/reader—all with the intent of having this exchange instill personal empowerment and initiate community development.

Why Consider Multimedia?

The strengths of multimedia are (1) their power to integrate complementary types of data that maximize users' experiences (whether for scholarly purposes or personal enjoyment), and (2) the relative ease with which they can be constructed and distributed (i.e., from a personal computer). At the same time, these can also be multimedia's greatest weaknesses. Poorly designed or constructed multimedia become that much more confusing, and these mismatched messages are then distributed online. As we have pointed out several times over, consider your intended audience and then design the project along the most appropriate and suitable conventions for this audience. If you do not, your product may have no impact whatsoever or, worse yet, be construed as misinformation. In short, the most effective multimedia are those that (1) integrate informative materials to enhance the experience rather than overburden the user, and (2) present these materials in ways and relationships that a linear format cannot. This seems obvious, right? So, in order to make quality multimedia, do not get distracted by all the bells and whistles, but simply focus on the quality of the content and the effective execution of its delivery. Whenever in doubt, keep it simple.

Blogs and Webpages

Webpages developed using hypertext markup language (HTML), which represented the cutting edge of web-based visual communication from the late 1990s through the early 2000s. Today, the range of computer languages and applications for creating and managing a web-presence has expanded beyond what any one individual can master. The sophistication of web-based applications allows nonexperts to develop a web presence with word processing skills alone, and free accounts on sites such as Blogger, WordPress, and Tumblr simply require the ability to drag and drop to upload images. Realize that what you get for free often has limitations, so check what various sites charge for long-term service and what added functionality they provide. Universities may also provide space for professional or class-related websites (and may even help you support it). Also note that unless you want to use the domain name designated by the provider, you should purchase a personal domain name (search online for vendors).

For visual researchers, blogs and webpages represent excellent means for communicating with your (a) research community, (b) colleagues, and (c) funding agencies. Regular updates can keep relevant audiences interested and connected to you and your work. However, easy as it may be to start a blog, know that maintaining one is a great deal of work and that the amount of content you plan to provide determines the amount of time required. If you plan to post field notes, at the least be sure to edit them before placing them online, both to protect yourself and the people with whom you work. While we recognize that blogs may serve as a forum for research writing and reflection, we recommend using the utmost discretion in deciding what and how content is posted and presented. Check with your participants to find out if they are interested in being a part of the blog or webpage. If not, refrain from doing it. Finally, when considering a webpage or blog for your work, think about your audience and how you want them to interact with your site. For example, are you interested in them only being aware of your work, or do you want their comments and responses? Blogs are relatively informal and invite reader feedback, so they are great if you want to elicit virtual engagement with your research (such as even through a Facebook page). If not, it is important to consider just who could read your blog and if the materials you post could have negative consequences.[5]

As visual researchers we (Marion and Crowder) think about having a web presence where people can see our work, but not see *all* of our work. We choose representative images to illustrate what we do and then provide the context for those images. For your own work, then, seriously consider which images you make available, as you could find them picked up and used by others for very different purposes than you originally intended. This can have ethical ramifications (as discussed in Chapter 1) and can jeopardize your fieldwork relationships. To state it clearly, a little forethought can save you a lot of grief. All of these considerations also apply to any video content you choose to use, whether embedded in your site itself or linked from Vimeo or YouTube to add another dimension to your work. Again, keep your audience in mind when selecting videos to enhance your site.

Digital Storytelling

Where webs and blogs are geared toward displaying and communicating research materials with a broad audience, digital stories are focused, multimedia productions that concentrate on one person's narrative. Most often these are created through workshops in which participants write a compelling personal account to which they add images, text, audio (voice-over) and video. Digital stories are short multimedia pieces, usually two to three minutes in length (eight at most). These stories are typically created to tell someone's intimate story, usually about meaningful episodes in his or her life that are meant to resonate with others. Digital storytelling has been employed in Community-Based Participatory Research (CBPR) projects (e.g., Gubrium 2009) in such domains as public health, ethnography, and the humanities. Digital stories do not require much more than free movie making software, personal photographs, and public domain music, although from there they can very quickly become much more sophisticated (see Lambert 2009). Depending upon the subject matter, once digital stories are created, they can then be placed on the Internet and shared with audiences ranging from local to global communities.

Figure 7.2 StarCAVE: Demonstrating the StarCAVE, Thomas DeFanti (University of California San Diego) shows visitors a high-definition, three-dimensional 360-degree image of the Temple at Luxor made with his three-dimensional CAVEcam during a proof-of-concept excursion to Egypt in April 2011. The StarCAVE—a virtual reality environment at Calit2 where researchers can engage with images (still or video) while wearing passive three-dimensional glasses—consists of five walls with three screens each, plus floor projection. In all, the environment requires thirty-four projectors (a polarized pair for each screen) and eighteen computers to render images wherein the viewer(s) can be completely immersed. ©2011 John Hanacek/Calit2 University of California at San Diego. (Color original.)

The Role of Multimedia in Research

By definition, multimedia blends various forms of content (audio, video, text, interactivity) into one product or piece that can be viewed across platforms (online, television, computer, etc.). For researchers, multimedia is an excellent means for conducting research, crafting a message, engaging an audience, and creating a story about the people (or other subjects) with whom you work. Knowing the audience for your multimedia project will help you keep the message focused.

Good multimedia should seamlessly provide the context within which the user/viewer can experience your findings and conclusions without having to pay attention to how you have tried to generate that particular experience. When starting out, we recommend avoiding extravagant multimedia projects. Because the learning curve for these endeavors can be quite steep, seek training or partners who know what they are doing. Misusing multimedia jeopardizes audience interest, as well as potential funding, and wastes the time you invest. While slick multimedia productions may entice (and even convince), remember that a great deal of work, time, and effort go into making them appear that way. Even though digital technologies make it easier for us to craft multimedia projects from our desktops, a certain level of skill[6] and a lot of thought is required to make the most of the technology. Kate Hennessy's case study in this chapter exemplifies the powerful possibilities for working with multimedia in cultural research based on long-term, thoughtful, and collaborative visualization efforts.[7] An entirely different but equally exciting example of the capacity to convey broad context through multimedia comes from cyber-archaeology—such as the work of the Cyber-Archaeology group, at the Calit2 Center of Interdisciplinary Science for Art, Architecture, and Archaeology at the University of California San Diego[8]—wherein visualizations (as seen in Figure 7.2) facilitate virtual exploration and excavation.

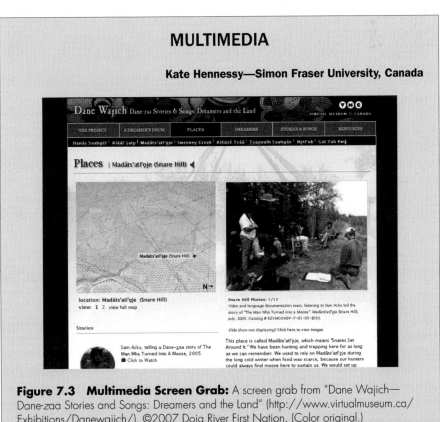

MULTIMEDIA

Kate Hennessy—Simon Fraser University, Canada

Figure 7.3   Multimedia Screen Grab: A screen grab from "Dane Wajich— Dane-zaa Stories and Songs: Dreamers and the Land" (http://www.virtualmuseum.ca/ Exhibitions/Danewajich/). ©2007 Doig River First Nation. (Color original.)

New technologies have transformed the ways in which ethnographic media can be documented, archived, viewed, and accessed. Yet one of the most significant things I have come to understand in my work in digital ethnography with First Nations

91

and Aboriginal communities in Canada is that the *process* of producing media is as important—if not more so—than the final product itself. For me this has meant placing collaboration with my research partners centrally in the creation of digital ethnography and new media forms. While our production process eventually results in a complete multimedia work, the ethnographic and technical insights gained in the course of our work together makes these projects particularly worthwhile.

In the participatory production of the virtual exhibit *Dane Wajich—Dane-zaa Stories and Songs: Dreamers and the Land*,[9] for example, our team was privileged to be guided by Dane-zaa elders who determined which oral histories should be recorded, and where we should travel in their territory to document them. We worked together to curate archival photographs and record new media that would tell the story of Dane-zaa Prophets and the songs that they passed down to present generations. However, in the process of producing the website, we also had to evaluate the cultural appropriateness of publically circulating sensitive or sacred documentation of cultural knowledge online. This resulted in the removal of some of the exhibit content, but also the generation of new collective understanding of local cultural property rights and the limitations of the Internet in safeguarding cultural heritage.

In another example, the virtual exhibit and archive *Inuvialuit Living History*[10] was designed to make an Inuvialuit collection at the Smithsonian Institution more accessible to originating communities so that the objects could become a part of daily life in new forms. For our team—which included Inuvialuit community members, Smithsonian curators, archaeologists, filmmakers, educators, and computer programmers—many of our greatest insights emerged in the iterative process of collaborative design. We learned about institutional and community relations of power, systems of media ownership and copyright, and issues of repatriation of cultural property. I view the design of ethnographic multimedia as a significant opportunity to tease out expressions of knowledge and power that are as embedded in digital code as they're in our research methodologies and disciplinary structures.

Summary

Historically, researchers have relied upon linear means for presenting their material whether in printed or visual formats. The digital revolution allows text, audio, images, and video to be combined in nonlinear forms such as webpages and hypermedia wherein the user navigates through the materials. Currently multimedia is the most common (albeit not necessarily the most well accepted) means of popularizing research, but less often a topic of research in itself.[11] Recognizing the strengths and weaknesses of different formats—from simple PowerPoint presentations to sophisticated web designs—this chapter highlighted the importance of matching multimedia to specific ends and audiences. Whether a poster or digital story, what do you want the audience to experience? Think through how the various types of content and effects interact; do they complement or clash with each other? A great deal of thought, time, and energy are required for developing multimedia that are effective in describing your research and maintaining your audience's attention. For example, overly dramatic music and voice-overs, fancy transitions and fades, unstable camera work, and garbled sound all distract the viewer from the message and focus their attention on the poor production of the piece. The bottom line with multimedia is to keep it as complete and seamless as possible.

Further Readings and Resources

- *The Future of Visual Anthropology* (Pink 2006)
- "Elementary Forms of the Digital Media: Tools for Applied Action Collaboration and Research in Visual Anthropology" (Biella 2009b)
- "Interactive Media in Anthropology: Seed and Earth—Promise of Rain" (Biella 1996)
- "Living Avatars Network: Fusing Traditional and Innovative Ethnographic Methods Through a Real-time Mobile Video Service" (Denisa and Graham 2010)
- "The Somali Bantu Experience: Using Multimedia Ethnography for Community Building, Public Education and Advocacy" (Besteman 2009)
- The journal *Visual Studies* has a regular section called "New Media Review," which frequently considers multimedia productions

Section 3

USING IMAGES

8

ORGANIZATION AND STORAGE

(a.k.a. "Where's My Stuff?")
with Michele Reilly

In this chapter you will learn about:

- How to develop a workflow to organize your digital files based on your own needs
- The basics of file organization
- How to assess which types of storage may work best for your work needs
- The value of archiving digital data

A common issue for people working with digital data is keeping them organized in order to find them later.[1] After all, if you cannot find an image or a file, how can you use it? This chapter is designed to introduce you to overarching ideas about organization and storage from which you can develop your own system for organizing your digital files. Ultimately we want you to be more efficient and accurate in your work, allowing you to spend less time looking for your files and more time working with them. Because we are focusing on organization, the ideas presented are (a) about making it easier for you to later retrieve and use your images, and (b) just as applicable whether you are working with new images or are scanning your old research photos or film to digital files.

Before we move forward, we want to define a few terms that will be used throughout the remainder of the book, especially as these definitions clarify how we approach organizing and working with digital files.

- **Database:** any mechanism that allows you to gather descriptive information (e.g., spreadsheets, access databases, software enhancements that come with your computer operating system, photo editing software)
- **Backup:** saving your work on a regular basis
- **Program:** photo editing software

- **Image Treatment:** the manipulation of images (e.g., such as color correcting and cropping)
- **Editing:** the process of selecting and manipulating images
- **Archiving:** managing files for long-term storage and enduring accessibility

Workflow

The technical term "workflow" is derived from the software and publishing industries that used it to depict how a process is manifested in the various steps involved from concept to product. It is also a common term used in the imaging world because of this exact exercise. Not all workflows are the same, and they tend to be most useful when they are simple. Developing the workflow that is right for you may take several iterations, but once you have got it you will be organized with a process and structure to protect your data now and for the future.

Think of workflow as a ritual, something you do the same way each time to ensure that the desired outcome is always met. Having a viable, dependable routine for processing your digital data protects you from forgetting anything and keeps you organized. Furthermore, if you find that you did make a mistake, you can more easily backtrack through the process to find where that occurred. Workflows can be as detailed and elaborate as you want, or as simple and uncomplicated as you need. In any case, however, we want to stress that once you have a process you are comfortable with, stick with it.

For ease of reference, Crowder keeps an abridged version of his workflow on a sticky note hanging from his computer monitor that he can refer to it each time he begins moving files from a device (e.g., camera, voice recorder, etc.) to his desktop. Having that little reminder at hand is nice, no matter how many times you have performed the steps. Think of your workflow as following a favorite recipe: It is always nice to have the cookbook at hand, even if you consult it but rarely. The steps on Crowder's sticky note that guide his workflow are **copy**, **rename**, **image treatment** (IT), **optimize, backup.** While there are some intermediary steps, this sticky note schematic provides a guideline. Crowder knows what to do in order to get to each next step. As we have been stressing throughout this book, there are many ways to work with digital data, so use the information below to help you conceptualize and create the workflow that best fits *your* needs. In Figure 8.1, we provide an example of a workflow that begins with a RAW image and ends with a JPEG file for publication—including backing up along the way.

Copy

When you are ready to transfer files from your device (e.g., camera, digital media card), or scanning photos to your computer, consider these steps. First, create a

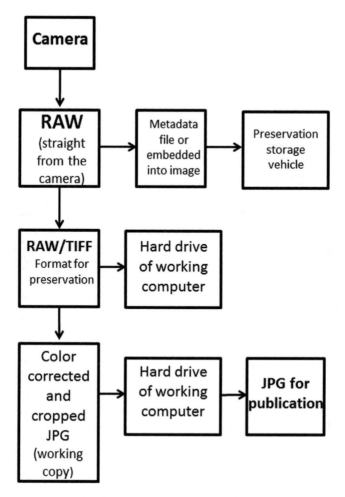

Figure 8.1   RAW→JPEG: This flowchart illustrates the steps involved in taking a RAW image from your camera through the processes of making it into a JPEG for publication.

destination folder on your desktop and name it appropriately (so you cannot later confuse it with other folders). Using a short, relevant term and the year (e.g., montreal 2011, smith 09[2]) works well, so you immediately have a reference as to the contents (and the temporal origin) of the folder. After creating the destination folder, *copy* the files from the source to your destination folder. We recommend that you copy *all* of the files to this folder—even the bad ones—so you have a complete copy of your work on the desktop. Remember, images are data. The worst picture may be the most ethnographically significant!

If you have heard it once, we are here to reiterate it: After you follow the renaming process, *back up* your files! Before you open the file to admire your work, *copy* this folder to an external drive or disc. Do not consider this *copy* as a waste of space or

Figure 8.2 1, 2, 3: The tree figure details some simple steps for taking images from your camera to backing them up on an external drive.

of a disc. These media are cheap, is your research? Creating file backups (Figure 8.2) prevents you from losing your images (data) if anything should happen to your computer or device, and it is a place to begin again if your files become corrupted. Never forget, having a backup copy may save you later! This is essential to good file management and data safety. An important related point is to *never* work on *original* files—that is why you have copies. The files you copied become your backup copy, while the files on your desktop will be the ones you will work with. As a simple rule, always have *at least* two copies of your photos; or three for the paranoid or the cautious.

Name (Nomenclature)

Every digital device has a default naming convention. These vary by manufacturer, type of device, and the type of output file that it creates. For example, your camera may create filenames like "DSCF0001" or "IMG001." What do these mean? Not much! They're generic referents that over time can become quite confusing as duplicate filenames get copied onto your computer. So, once you have copied the files onto your computer—and backed up—it is time to open them using dedicated programs (a free one may have come with your camera). The task now is to *(re)name* your files to always be findable by using names that will help you organize your data. The single best way to do this is by maintaining a sequential numbering system throughout the folder, especially as you (may) continue to add images over time.

We cannot stress this enough: *Naming your images is the most important step in the workflow process.* It requires some consideration on your part before moving ahead, but ensures that you will never duplicate a filename. Once you have renamed your working images, it is time to make a copy of your renamed images. This backup copy can now serve as your go-to file if your working files ever get corrupted. As with all backing up, these files/folders copies should be saved onto external hard drives, flash drives, or discs.

Batch

Arguably the most useful tool found in many photo editing programs is the batch editing function. This simple tool allows you to rename *all* of your images simultaneously (i.e., without having to rename each image individually). Because there are so many programs available, you should consult the "Help" file for your particular application. Performing batch operations will (a) save you time and (b) allow you to be consistent throughout the file. Also note that batch commands help when resizing, optimizing, or placing watermarks on your image files. Do not, however, use batch commands for image treatment (e.g., color correction, cropping); these functions require individual consideration. Finally, so you can find your images later, keep your naming conventions consistent throughout the folders, subfolders, and images within the subfolders. Figure 8.3 leads you through an example of the steps for creating folders and renaming your images.

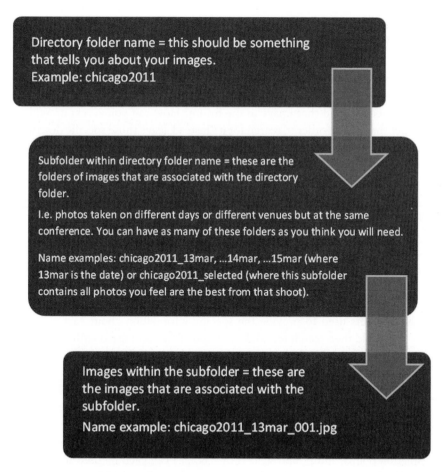

Figure 8.3 Folders Within Folders: This graphic shows one process for naming folders and (re)naming images in subfolders.

We know the impulse to immediately start working with your images can feel irresistible (we have been there), but taking the time to set up your file management (see Figure 8.4) from the outset will save you future headaches if anything should happen to your images. (We have been here too, which is part of how we learned.) Also realize that the redundancy achieved by placing the date in the file name, along with the information automatically placed in the file by the device (in the metadata), is not superfluous. Indeed it can be quite important because when you process images—specifically, changing their format or size—the embedded metadata can be deleted. You may not consider this a problem now, but if you need to find specific images in five years you will appreciate a systematic naming procedure. When you have to find those images, having the date in both the folder and file name greatly facilitates such searches.

Subfolders

Often people rename pictures to refer to that specific image (e.g., "Jack speaking at AAA"). This title may seem well and good in the moment, but what about when you need to find that image in the future? How can you access it? Will you remember that title in order to search for it? Instead, leave those specific descriptors out of the file name and create a name that is both *short and informative*. Remember, not all computers will allow for long file names so brevity, conciseness, and consistency are of key importance. For example, an image of Jack speaking at the 2010 American Anthropology Association meetings could sloppily be labeled "Jack speaking at AAA." But that type of filename doesn't help when you need to find it again among folders, or even multiple hard drives, full of images. Instead the image could be named as one of the images shot during that meeting overall (e.g., folder name: aaa_2010) and the files may be sequentially ordered (e.g., aaa_2010_001, aaa_2010_002, etc.). The photo of Jack speaking is just one of many, and your *database*—where you tag, rate, and rank your images according to whatever criteria you choose—gets used to provide the specific information about each particular image. You could then search for "Jack" and find all images tagged with "Jack." Once you find the ones you like best, copy them to a "keepers/select" subfolder.

One tip we would like to offer is not to be afraid of using special characters to help organize titles or separate information within the filename. While many in the computer industry frown on the use of special characters (because of inherent conflicts with specific operating systems and server types) we have never found this to be a problem when using a basic PC or Apple computer. En dashes, ampersands, exclamation points, and pound signs (i.e., -, &,!, #) can each be used to symbolize special file characteristics. And here is the key: As long as you are consistent, you can

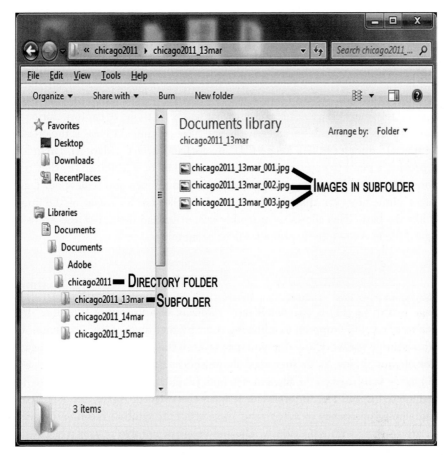

Figure 8.4 Organizational Integrity: This screen capture illustrates the tree-like structure of a good filing system, including the mother folder (directory) with the daughter folder (subfolder) that contains the images. Such nesting of folders is an appropriate means for keeping all of your images/videos organized within one main folder.

use them however you want. After adjusting the brightness or color of an image, for instance, you may place an ampersand (&) following the file number, so you know it has been processed and is not the original. Similarly, you could place a pound sign (#) after the number if you crop an image, or use an exclamation point (!) to note an image you particularly like. What and how you name your files is up to you; there is no one right way to do this. What is important to remember is (a) to be *consistent* in your naming conventions and (b) to keep it *simple*. Also note that it is *always* a good idea to make a *key* for yourself (and others) to keep track of the symbols you are using and their meanings.

Selection

Selecting images is an ongoing process, as you will approach your collection with different needs and intents on different occasions. Basic editing requires that you open your program in a browsing mode, where you view and scroll through thumbnails of your images.[3] Your first pass or two through the collection may simply be to select[4] the images that best represent what you were trying to capture during the shoot. One habit we each began early on, and have continued to use, is the creation of a special subfolder called "keepers" (Crowder) and "select" (Marion). These folders provide a place to copy *all* of the images we liked or selected so (a) they're all in one place, and (b) we do not necessarily have to re-open and review our tagged images. Note, however, that the "keepers/select" files are for *copies* of the images we like the best.[5] This allows us to readily save or upload them, but also keeps the original file in context in its primary folder or subfolder.

Image Treatment

Image treatment (IT) is an overall term referring to a variety of functions, from basic rotating[6] and cropping to adjusting color balance and red-eye reduction. It is at this point in the workflow that you may want to start cropping or color balancing some of your photos. As we suggested above, choose specific characters (e.g.,!, @, #, $,%) to use as suffixes on the filenames to both (a) indicate specifically how you have manipulated it and (b) differentiate it from the original. Again, the key here is maintaining consistency so you always know what the symbols mean and whether you are working with a previously adjusted image or not. No matter what, *always work on a copy of your photo.* Never edit the original!

If you decide to crop or color balance, there are a few important things to consider. To **crop** an image means to *relimit* it—or define new boundaries of the photograph—effectively reformatting it. Photo editing programs provide tools that help crop for specific print sizes and formats (e.g., 4 × 6 in., 200 × 250 mm) that may not match the aspect ratio of the sensor in your digital camera. As such, if you were to print your digital photographs as you took them, the resulting prints might have thick white borders, or other telltales of the mismatch between the aspect ratios of the sensor and the paper. As noted in Chapter 5, digital sensors come in a variety of sizes, so you may well need to crop your images depending upon the size you wish to print them.

Color correction is achieved in multiple ways and is beyond the scope of this book to cover in detail (but see the references listed at the end of this chapter). The basic tool set for color correction includes: lines, curves, hue, saturation, contrast, and highlights. You can use any single tool, or any combination of them, to adjust an image's color. Whatever you do, though, do not forget to indicate the change in the filename as you correct each image.

Metadata (What to Consider)

The third pass through your folder is a good time to start attaching descriptors to the images. Descriptive text that you place in the database is called metadata, and can include fields for where each image was shot, the names of the people in the images, notes about the context of what was taking place, and so forth.[7] Metadata make visual content easily accessible through words, terms, or through machine-readable codes and strings. Metadata are the descriptors of an image connected to it through a database; qualitative researchers often call these codes.

There are two basic types of metadata, *embedded* and *self-generated*. Embedded metadata usually include technical aspects of the image (e.g., f-stop, shutter speed, focal length, date and time the image was taken). Self-generated metadata are those inputted by the user (e.g., keywords, names, notes, copyrights). Chapter 9 addresses metadata in greater depth since metadata really help in exploring our images more than organizing them. What *is* important organizationally, however, is that metadata provide opportunities to directly connect images with their contexts and pertinent qualitative information. If you take the time to properly enter information into the metadata fields, the organized combination of image and text becomes a power-ful tool. For example, using the search function of the database allows us to find images and relationships between images we may never have considered. Just as importantly (even if more superficially), we can immediately find images by people, places, dates, or times, depending upon our needs.

Optimize, Resize, Reformat

There are several reasons to optimize and resize your images, including (but not limited to) making them easier to share, use, and maintain. Large image files are often clumsy and unnecessary, especially when being viewed on a monitor or projector—where large file sizes simply require more memory and loading time. Also realize that larger files do not necessarily look any better on a monitor than a smaller file, as their resolution depends upon the number of pixels per inch (ppi).[8] Furthermore, sharing large image files with colleagues or friends without knowing exactly how they'll use them (or the hardware they'll use to open them), can prove problematic (e.g., clogging inboxes).[9] As such, it's a good idea never to send large files from the outset, but to provide images that are easily viewable (but not neces-sarily printable or otherwise usable).[10]

It is important to optimize your images for the specific task, whether attaching them to an e-mail, including them in a slide show, or preparing them for print. Optimizing your images effectively protects you from providing files that are inac-cessible or unusable. To **optimize**, in this sense, means making the file appropriate for its use, which in most instances involves resizing them to be smaller and easier to transfer or display (e.g., e-mailing, projecting). To resize your images you can return to the batch function to process all of the selected images so that they are all the same size and resolution. As you optimize and resize, place the smaller images in a subfolder named to denote this change from the original (e.g., "optimized"). If you resize your images for various uses—say, printing, electronic sharing, and presentations—be sure to keep track of which images have been optimized in which ways (i.e., in different subfolders, or with different suffixes, like "@72"). To summarize some of the key ideas regarding resizing and optimizing images:

- Place the images in their own appropriately labeled subfolder
- Crop them to the appropriate size and resolution for their purpose
  o Use the batch function to resize and optimize multiple images
- Change the image names to denote the resizing

Reformatting is changing the digital image from one format (i.e., file type) into another; for example, from a TIFF to a JPEG. While this short text cannot dedicate much ink to discuss scanning film or photos, many readers may have large archives of print or celluloid media to be digitized. If this is you, try to create as large a file as possible when importing the image, as doing so allows you to retain the most information (data) about that image. Be aware that scans can create very large files (e.g., from 20 to more than 68 megabytes each), which, while excellent for archiving, are not so terrific for placing in a presentation or on a digital frame. So, create an uncompressed file when you scan (usually a TIFF), which will facilitate printing large photos that retain detailed information. For use on a monitor or projector, however, you should *reformat* (i.e., convert) them to a compressed file format, the most popular of which is JPG, JPEG, and JPG2000. Compressed files have enough information in them to look good on the screen, but not usually enough to make high-quality prints, as they have been compressed. Again, your program can perform this action via the batch command, and placing them in an appropriately labeled subfolder keeps all of the images together and easy to find.

Export

Although Chapter 10 is dedicated to *using* your images, it is exporting, the last step in the workflow, that gets you to that point. The term "exporting" means sending your images from the program into a folder someplace else, for example, in an online gallery, in a slide presentation, in an application such as PowerPoint or Keynote, or in a digital photo frame. Being clear about how you want to use the images is a strong motivator for sizing the images correctly. As already noted, carrying around overstuffed PowerPoint files on a flash drive or trying to e-mail large image files to colleagues (or family) can be frustrating and time-consuming. You can create files within your project folder for just this purpose.[11] For example, if you are building a slideshow for a lecture, you know that you will need the images to be at

72 dpi and probably no larger than 8 x 10 in. Resizing the images to fit those dimensions will create smaller files you can then easily export to a PowerPoint-like application.[12] In Chapter 10, we will discuss creating effective and simple presentations. Of course the Internet is quickly becoming the place for exporting images to share with friends, colleagues, research participants, and others. This segues well into the next section of the chapter that specifically deals with preparing your images for various types of storage and archiving.

Storage and Archiving

Storage and archiving are not the same. Storage refers to keeping images available for easy access. These can be images you currently work with, have worked on, or may work with that are stored locally: either on an internal hard drive, external hard drive, digital optical disc (CD-ROM or DVD-ROM), or flash drive. Archiving is not about current activity or concerns. The purpose of archiving is to preserve your images for use over time, that is, in a format that will be available in ten, fifteen, twenty-five or even a hundred years (you choose). Do not assume that just because you have burned a DVD-ROM of your images (for a particular event) that they are then archived. Far from it. If you place that same disc in your computer a few years from now you will see data loss (also known as bit rot or data rot).

This last section of the chapter concentrates on strategies for storing your work and archiving your files. Taking the former into consideration, you realize that storage is a dynamic process and you can move and copy files between various media with the implicit understanding that none of them are permanent. Therefore, your decisions about storage will change, both depending upon the context of the work and as your needs develop over time. On the other hand, the decisions you make now regarding archiving digital data will affect you for a very long time. As such, you need to think through (a) exactly what you want to do with the data you plan to archive, and (b) what you are willing to spend in order to do that.

Storage

The *cloud* will be the most useful place to store (but not archive) your images both now and in the future. You may place your images in free or for-pay space on the Internet with the idea that you will have access to them whenever you want so long as you have an Internet connection). Still, depending where you go you may have limited bandwidth, so uploading and downloading files to the cloud may not be too dependable. Again, if you are only trying to post your images for others to look at (e.g., Facebook, Snapfish, Flickr, or Picasa), you will want to size them accordingly— not only for monitor resolution, but also to be small enough that they easily upload and do not fall victim to poor Internet connectivity or bandwidth.[13]

Be aware and be careful: Internet storage companies come and go. Trusting your original (nonbacked up) images to an Internet company is placing your images at risk. For the past decade the easiest, and perhaps cheapest, means for storing images have been digital optical discs, either CD-ROM or DVD-ROM. These are still very viable media for storage, with the drawbacks of limited capacity and read/write speed (e.g., 8X, 24X, 48X). Also, realize that DVDs *do not last forever* (and maybe not even a few years). This is not a problem if you are using them as a means of temporary back up, but think ahead and be sure to find an alternative that will allow for storage longevity. Likewise, keep in mind that optical discs degrade over time, so they should never be your only strategy for storage or backing up data.

Today, with the ongoing development of larger and larger hard drives (external, internal, portable, and flash) it is very easy to store large amounts of data quickly and reliably. Large video, photo, and audio files can be cumbersome to access via optical discs, but are much easier to access when placed on a hard drive. For the past decade the standard interfaces have been USB and FireWire (each with its own specific interface/connector). At the time of this printing, new technologies have come online that significantly boost the speed at which these drives and your computer communicate to effectively transfer data.[14] FireWire 800 (Apple), Thunderbolt (Apple), eSATA, and USB 3.0[15] will all be in use for at least a few years to come, each with its own advantages and disadvantages.

This is not the place to discuss these interfaces in detail, but when you price external drives, carefully consider your options at each price point. Especially as time marches on, some of these technologies will become obsolete. So keep your data viable by having multiple interfaces on your drive (e.g., USB 3.0 and eSATA or USB 2.0 and FireWire 800). A drive that hosts several types of interfaces is also a very good idea, as it will help ensure you do not get locked out of accessing data in the future. Also note that some external drives feature network access (via CAT-6), which means that as long as you leave them on and connected to your network, you can access them from the Internet via an Ethernet interface.[16]

While we promote hard drives as efficient and relatively inexpensive storage devices, it is crucial to remember that these are mechanical and will eventually fail. Technology now provides solid-state, dependable drives available as internal and external drives for your computer, as well as in portable form (e.g., your CF, SD, HDSC, and XD digital camera discs). USB flash drives—also known as jump drives or thumb drives—offer a relatively large capacity in a small and durable device.[17] Furthermore, the same technology appears in larger formats that can be placed into your laptop or desktop (decreasing noise, heat, and energy consumption). Compare this to how CD and DVDs were stored in the 1990s and 2000s, in large, bulky binders or jewel cases. Now, exponentially more data gets stored in cases hundreds of times smaller, and in the coming years more and more storage will likely depend on the cloud (versus physical storage).

We move into a completely different realm when we consider archiving digital data. Our incessant plea to *back up* your work data becomes a constant drone when archiving, as the discussion no longer concerns amounts of storage, but longevity and the retrieval of data. Archiving is about storing originals rather than working files or copies. Your archived file is the unadulterated file—without any processing (e.g., compression, cropping, color balance)—that you can return to if and when you need to see it. When it comes to archiving, you cannot settle for "good enough" since digital storage has not been around long enough to even know what that really means! If you do not care for your originals, what can you expect to have in the future?

Archiving relies upon recoverability and reproducibility in the future. You have to ask yourself, "How will I access this file in ten years, in fifteen years?" This question points to the interface, the media, and the file type. As we have seen over the years, print, image, sound, and movie formats have changed drastically. The progress of each format is illustrated in Figure 8.5.

Formats for Archiving

When scanning printed photos you should always make TIFF files, as these are rarely compressed and are considered the standard when RAW images are not available. (Some companies claim to create RAW files from scans, but they do not

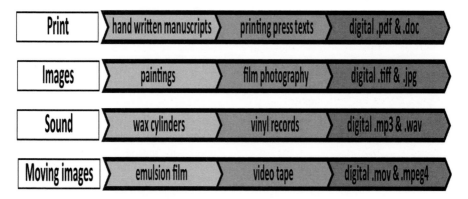

Figure 8.5 Evolving Formats: This graphic depicts how various media formats have progressed over time. It also illustrates the use of shapes and shading for adding visual emphasis to text-based content.

behave like camera-generated RAW files). For digital photos, RAW is preferred but a TIFF file will do. One caveat is not to archive your JPEG files unless that is the *only* format you have of the file. Creating a TIFF out of a JPEG is not normally a good idea, nor will it really improve the quality of your file. Like many processes, the adage, "garbage in, garbage out" holds true, so do not expect much if you try to make larger files from compressed ones. As with photos, you should always shoot video at the optimum quality possible, archive the original files, and then compress it to produce working files.

Because large external hard drives have become widely available and relatively cheap, an option that may work for a time would be to use the largest drive you can afford upon which you store your data once and then just turn it off and lock it in your closet. The longer your drives are on and spinning, the shorter their lifespan. Infrequently using a disc to store your originals and keeping it unplugged and safe is a form of dark storage—dark meaning that the machine is turned off. If you were to be hypervigilant about this method, you could rotate two more drives in this process, effectively copying new work to every other one, so that there is always redundancy. By following a preset workflow, choosing file formats wisely, maintaining multiple copies in various types of drives and media (Table 8.1), keeping files in

Table 8.1 Storage Media.

	Storage Type (in order of max capacity)	Pros	Cons	Future (in order of obselesance)
SMALLEST	Optical (CD/DVD/BLU-Ray)	inexpensive, ubiquotous interface	slow read/write speed, size, portability, longevity, single use	storage
	Flash drive (USB)	inexpensive, small size, unbiqutous interface, fast read/write, longevity, large capacity	easy to lose, data security	portable storage
	Spinning disc (hard drive)	multiple interfaces, large capacity	expensive, size:weight, electrical needs, slow read/write speeds	dark storage, archiving
GREATEST	Cloud	unlimited size, inexpensive, ubiqutous, shareable	internet accessible only, speed determined by internet access	storage, limited archiving

different states of revision, archiving open source or industry standard formats you will help ensure the long term usability of your images.[18]

Finally, five key things to keep in mind when working with your computer are:

1. Always use passwords to secure your data.
2. Plug all of your computer equipment into a power strip or surge protector at all times, or better yet, an Uninterruptible Power Supply (UPS), if possible.
3. Use antivirus, spyware, and malware programs to protect your computer.
4. Always update your software.
5. BACK UP YOUR DATA!

DIGITAL ARCHIVING

Michele Reilly—University of Houston, United States

About ten years ago the standards for digital archiving and conversion were in their infancy. At the University of Houston we were presented with a large collection of sound recordings on a medium that was rapidly becoming inaccessible: reel-to-reel audiotape. We determined that these materials needed to be reformatted and archived soon and in a way that would ensure long-term usability and access. At the time, converting these sound recordings to two copies on CD and one copy on reel-to-reel was the industry standard. Today, we would simply make these materials available online and archive them to spinning disc for dark storage (hard drives). When we began the process of transferring these digital files from the ten-year-old CDs, we found that some of the CDs would not open, others were missing data, and others had no data (due to data rot). Given that level of data loss, we had to send the reel-to-reel tapes that corresponded to the corrupt CDs to a transfer company and reprocess them. At that point, file naming became the issue because the digital file names did not match the file names on the reel-to-reel tapes. We did have a key, so narrowing it down to a few reel-to-reel tapes was possible, but matching the exact digital files to an exact reel was impossible. Not only did this cost us time to decipher the provenance of the files, but it cost us even more money to retransfer the audio to digital file format! With that in mind we established a standard for our archive, normalizing the file names across all the types of media, copying all files to spinning disc, hosting all files online, and adding written notes into our metadata to ensure provenance of the transfers between media. Our situation could have been much worse had industry standards not been followed ten years earlier. Doing that ensured that a nuisance was not a disaster.

Summary

This chapter emphasized the need to create a consistent and organized workflow for taking your images from your camera to your computer. Here we covered the various steps you should consider when developing your own workflow and discuss the most basic concepts, which are copy, rename, image treatment, optimization, and backing up. For each concept we explained the how and why, providing examples to clarify exactly what we mean. Renaming your files is the most important step because the way in which you do so will affect how you categorize and find them in the future. Even so, if there is one thing to remember from this chapter: Do not forget to back up your files. With that in mind, we also covered the differences between storage and archiving your files, and what you should consider when doing either. Lastly, we provided a table to help you identify the most appropriate types of media for your storage and archival needs.

Further Readings and Resources

- *Digital Photography Best Practices and Workflow Handbook: A Guide to Staying Ahead of the Workflow Curve* (Russotti and Anderson 2009)
- *The Digital Photography Workflow Handbook: From Import to Output* (Steinmueller and Gulbins 2010)
- "Media Convergence/Management Change: The Evolving Workflow for Visual Journalists" (Zavoina and Reichert 2000)
- "Review of Image and Video Indexing Techniques" (Idris and Panchanathan 1997)
- Digital Darkroom Resource CD-ROM, 3rd edition (Brooks 2011)
  - Also see Brooks' blog: https://sites.google.com/site/davidbrooksfotografx

9

EXPLORING IMAGES

with Michele Reilly

In this chapter you will learn about:

- How to think about using metadata to help with organization and analysis
- How metadata can improve search techniques
- The role of secondary analysis and applications for exploring images

In the previous chapter we introduced the concept of a workflow: a routine for consistently moving your digital files from your device to your computer and effectively organizing them. Part of that discussion concerns the need to properly name your digital files to facilitate future retrieval and recognition. In this chapter we build on this organizational foundation, highlighting the advantages of writing metadata (notes) about your photo files, which are then searchable in your operating system and editing software.

One of the reasons we suggest not deleting any of your images (see Chapter 8) is because these "bad" or "useless" images may emerge as valuable data later, revealing something that you may not have thought about or been interested in earlier. As suggested in all qualitative methods courses, writing regular, thorough notes is the key to strong research. Here we offer you new places for those notes that potentially can be more powerful for you than writing simple notes in your word processor.

Metadata in all Digital Files

Metadata are descriptors of digital files, whether audio, video, or photo. There are three types of metadata:

1. Technical metadata, which describes aspects of how the image/source file was generated
2. Descriptive metadata, which describes the content of the object
3. Administrative metadata, which describes the use, rights, and context of the file.

Each digital device embeds certain types of data into every file it generates. These data include very useable references, such as the date and time the file was made, as well as more nuanced specifics like the f-stop or shutter speed of an image. The thing to remember is that when you record digitally, you are recording more than the image or audio file. Your digital device captures technical metadata about each file, and this data can be quite useful when organizing or analyzing your files in the future.

Of course there is more to metadata than the technical specifics of an image or another type of digital file. Metadata can also include where an image was taken, who is in the image, and what the occasion happened to be. Librarians and digital archivists build matrices or spreadsheets to account for the various descriptors or metadata that accompany their objects. (See Figure 9.1 for an example of a metadata matrix constructed to account for any digital format—audio, video or photo.) You may opt to build a spreadsheet to capture the metadata for your images. If you can keep your images organized, the matrix serves as a searchable and sortable database which can help you quickly identify files that may be most useful to you.

Using a common spreadsheet is a great way to enhance your metadata and to keep information readily at hand. Spreadsheets offer a systematic way to record information about each of your images that your camera and your image editing software cannot store. While spreadsheets are particularly good for sorting and searching, their biggest disadvantage is the time involved in recording each image's

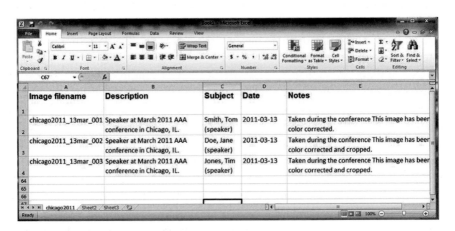

Figure 9.1   Sample Metadata Matrix: This is an example of a matrix for organizing metadata using a spreadsheet application. Note that the columns hold specific types of data for each image (place on the rows). Adding more columns allows you to capture more types of data. Think about how these can then cross-reference with your field notes.

metadata. One suggestion to this problem is to only enhance the metadata on the images you plan to use or have edited—then just remember to save this spreadsheet to the same subfolder as the images.

- Tip: Always include a field in your spreadsheet for the file name of each image. This will save time when you are trying to locate the image later.

While spreadsheets require coordination between the collection and the files themselves, the past decade has seen a dramatic improvement within programs to manage metadata embedded within the image files. Both public domain and purchasable applications have moved from storing all database information in separate proprietary spreadsheet files (hidden in the larger program) to embedding this information in the header portion of the image file itself.[1] This allows users to maintain the unique metadata with each image, so when it is copied or shared the corresponding data are moved with the file.

As mentioned above, there are various types of metadata embedded in an image. Briefly, there are two types that you may find when exploring metadata in your applications: Exchangeable Image File (EXIF) and International Press Telecommunications Council (IPTC). We mention them because it is important to understand which types of metadata are automatically embedded and which ones are not. EXIF is the term for technical metadata used by most digital cameras to describe the image, including image size, camera settings, date, and time. Usually these cannot be changed by the user, but are set by the camera and visible when open in the management application, or when viewed on the camera itself. These data will be accessed by the program, for example, when you ask it to find all images made within a particular time frame. The second type, IPTC, is a standard set of fields used to describe photographs. These fields offer the user an opportunity to input data such as a title, descriptions, author or creator name, image location, genre, and the like. In some cases, you can even enter multiple lines of text (i.e., notes).

Administrative metadata is a standard set of fields used to describe the rights and responsibilities of the object and its provenance. For ethnographers, this includes the copyright (whether you explicitly state it or not, if you made it, you own it), the date it was made, your ownership, and restrictions. Standard metadata schemes exist for digital files, which allow users a common lexicon for categorizing their files. One of the most well-known is called the Dublin Core. Another popular set of codes for ethnography can be found at the Human Relation Area Files (HRAF). Using a standard set of metadata terms and definitions makes your files more discoverable, findable, and assessable if you ever share them. In other words, interoperability—the ability to more easily share files with others who can then benefit from our work—is highly facilitated by the use of a shared set of codes.

As you become more familiar with your application you may find very power-ful ways to use metadata. One possibility is using the same codes in both text and image data. Then, when you conduct analysis, you can pull images as you find re-lationships in your field notes (or vice versa). This enhances the viability of your images, allowing them to become integrated with your text (and not just supple-mental material). As this option suggests, however, it is crucial to be consistent with your word choice when inputting your metadata. Some programs help the user by providing suggestions based upon words already placed in fields, which limits spell-ing mistakes and formatting inconsistencies (e.g., capitalization). Since inputting metadata is a long-term process, it is a good idea to keep a *code key*, much like that made for written field notes, so you do not substitute terms and maintain spelling consistencies (proper nouns can be especially tricky).

One exciting option to consider is that you do not need a database or image ed-iting software to tag your images with metadata, or even to perform viable searches. Your computer's operating system contains a powerful search engine and—like any other files indexed on the computer—will read file information from images and audio files. As such, taking time to input specific information about your images, videos, or audio recordings can greatly speed up and enhance the quality of future searches using your operating system's search engine alone. Making notes in the files about the nature of the images (such as identifying persons or noting places where recordings were made) prepares you to conduct basic analyses of your data. It also exponentially improves your ability to retrieve specific images and data whenever you may want to find them in the future (and may not even remember how they relate to your topic).

For example, when Crowder conducted an interview with a resident named Donald at his house, he used his digital voice recorder to capture the conversation and made use of a point-and-shoot camera to make a few images of Donald in his home that day. Also, when Donald went outside to show off his garden or described problems in the neighborhood, Crowder made photos of those things as well. Later, when Crowder copied the audio and image files to his desktop, he followed his work-flow, renaming them and saving them to an external hard drive (so they are safe).[2]

In Windows, he can then right-click on the audio file icon and scroll down to the bottom of the menu for Properties. Selecting Properties opens a box with tabs across the top, where he can view the descriptive fields (date/time, file size, file loca-tion) about the file. Clicking on the details tab accesses many empty fields divided into sections, including description, media, origin, content, and file. Working in the description section, he can give the file a subtitle (e.g., the project's name), rate the file (think of the possibilities for this feature), and place tags and comments in it.

These are useful fields for the researcher to place keywords for themes discussed during an interview, or even write a brief summary of the interview itself. Writing notes in this box immediately following an interview provides an opportunity to revisit the discussion and identify the most important parts of the conversation while it is still fresh in the researcher's mind. Like field notes, for example, Crowder can enter the location of where he spoke and who was present, so he has a record of the people whose voices (or any audio oddities) he may hear when he replays it later (and may not remember). Later, copying and pasting these notes to his field notes initiates the process of writing more detailed field notes, especially when and if Crowder decides to return to the file to transcribe it.[3] When he copies the file to his flash drive, or replaces the copy on his external hard drive, all of the data travels with it. At this moment you may not understand just how amazing this feature is for ethnographers (and other qualitative researchers) who rely upon their notes for accuracy and details. Filling the fields with details enables you to inquire more profoundly of the data later. Best of all, you do not need a fancy, expensive, sophisticated application; instead you just use the search engine in your operating system. Given the depth of your comments, you also may be able to discern whether you need to transcribe the interview or not. You can also note the timestamp so you can immediately return to an important part of the interview (and maybe only transcribe this portion).

Returning to the example of Donald, Crowder can later *search* to find all of the files dealing with Donald, or maybe "neighborhood conduct"—since this may be one of his tags and also appears in the comments section. Depending on the situation, Crowder may immediately burn a disc of photos for Donald on his laptop or return later and drop off the photos he took in Donald's garden and around the neighborhood. Crowder can take his laptop and show Donald all of the photos. At this moment Crowder should also capture the audio of their discussion.[4] As Donald speaks to the images, it is simple to fill-in the appropriate missing information regarding Donald's comments and thoughts. Again, Crowder can access these metadata by right-clicking the file's icon and exploring the file's properties (or edit the fields in an image management program). Jotting notes about each image as Donald speaks helps Crowder more accurately capture Donald's comments on the photos and also gives Crowder another opportunity to gather details he may have missed earlier.

Content

As briefly mentioned in Chapter 8, *content* data directly describe the image or the digital file, for example the date, time, place, and names of persons in the image. Content also includes descriptors of what is actually taking place in the image, such as "Julio harvesting potatoes in the Tiwanaku valley, village of Curva, May 2007." Content should be limited to describing the image itself and whatever is in the image. Appropriate content information in the metadata will allow you to search and compare images more easily, especially if you cross-reference your photos with your field notes.

Context

As qualitative researchers we want to emphasize the importance of context for any photo, video, or audio files. *Context,* in this sense, is a description of what was going on when you made the photo or video. Context captures all of the elements that affect the creation of your media file. These are not the obvious data, but instead are unique to the situation at hand. For example, bad weather could postpone a dance or a ritual, the family you work with could be fighting, or it may be a holiday and the kids are home from school. Even if you do not recognize its importance when you write it, situational context can play a huge role in your future analysis—providing information that helps inform analysis.

Search Techniques

The more information you place in your metadata fields, the more powerful your database will be for analysis. But placing too much text in metadata fields may yield inaccurate hits later, which means you waste time sifting through results for no reason. When conducting searches on your images (and accompanying metadata) keep in mind a few things:

* What is the question you are asking of your data?
* What are the appropriate terms you placed in the database?
* How much detail do you provide in order to resolve your questions?

Inappropriate, inaccurate, or insufficient metadata will not return much for you when you begin analyzing your images. Using a standard vocabulary across your metadata will ensure your searches result in fewer mistakes. Ethnographers may find the HRAF codes suitable but not exhaustive, but be sure to check out various online thesauri for controlled vocabularies that may work best for you.

Basic Searching

As the metadata are populated we can begin to conduct analysis on the images. Like searching any database, there are simple and complex ways to examine your images. Most programs have relatively strong search engines that will use a keyword, phrase, or tag—located in a folder or file name or other fields—to search across the platform (given the parameters you provide). Instead of using specific file names you can use strings of text (partial or complete) to locate the file. More advanced patterns may require a wildcard in place of a missing string of characters. Common wildcards include "?" and "*" to represent nonspecific characters in your search. For example:

- `<ja?.jpg>` could return `<jam.jpg>`, `<jan.jpg>` and `<jar.jpg>`, but not `<jack.jpg>`
- `<jam*.jpg>` could return `<jam.jpg>`, `<jams.jpg>` and `<jamos.jpg>`

Each application has its own quirks, so be sure to consult the help documentation for your program for more specifics on how the search function operates. Becoming familiar with how the search feature works will help you consider appropriate titles for folders and files and significantly expand the utility of your application. Besides using the search box of your application, you should also consider what are called selective searches or browsing. These begin with simple, embedded characteristics that help you immediately cull through your images, or other digital files, to land in the general vicinity of what you are looking for without limiting your parameters. In the following section, we consider when and how these strategies are effective and useful.

Chronological

Chronological searches provide a powerful means for locating images within a time range, logically, so you can browse those you took on certain days or weeks if you are trying to figure out when you visited a certain place or person, or coordinate your images with your field notes.[5] Management software, like Picasa, ACDSee, and even those that come bundled with your digital camera, provide very basic search and browsing functions. Most fundamental are those associated with the date and time stamp created when the image (or file) was first made. Since the timestamp is metadata (some programs allow you to change these dates), most searches are going to operate on the date and time in the file. Typically, applications provide date boxes or calendars so you can select the range of dates you are interested in searching. Alternatively, you may be presented a calendar upon which specific dates appear bold, signifying that there are photos in the database taken on those dates. When you select a day or week, thumbnails usually appear corresponding to the photos taken on those dates in the selected range.

Chronological browsing is useful when you need to insert metadata into a group of images, like those you took of Pierre in Paris—if you know about when you were with Pierre in Paris, then chronological browsing will help you readily find them. Once found, you can then select all of the images of Pierre and place his name as a keyword (as well as Paris), and any other appropriate information, so in future searches you can simply use his name and the city to find those images, and others of Pierre you may have. These basic searches are especially useful when (re)writing your field notes, as you can review content and context of the image(s) to enhance the details you provide in the notes; which may also remind you of specific conversations or issues discussed at that time, and other details. In this way the context associated with the image provides data you can place in your notes; often these are data you are only cognizant of in relation to the image itself.

Often during the selection process, when we are working through any set of im-ages we will tag the images we like most, for a variety of reasons. These usually are copied into our respective "keepers/select" subfolders for later use. In some programs to *tag* an image you only need to place a simple check mark in a box surrounding the thumbnail representation of the image. This Boolean (on/off) tag allows you to quickly identify the ones you like or those you want to use from those you do not. Once tagged, you can sort or inverse select to treat the images accordingly, like placing metadata.

Ranking your images adds levels of discrimination to your selection; no longer are we dealing with on/off values, but ranks. Some applications use the star system, and others provide circles with numbers or colors to differentiate between ranks. A number or star does not have to represent rank so to speak (i.e., those you like the best, second best, etc.), but instead can represent concepts or people, so you can quickly browse or sort without having their corresponding keywords embedded (yet). For example, when editing a group of images for an exhibit, Crowder will first pull in all of the images he is considering and then go through them to identify those that:

1. Must be included
2. He likes, but which may not help tell the story
3. Tell the story but may not be as visually strong as those ranked one or two
4. Other people suggest
5. He wants to compare with the rest, but does not consider "keepers" for the final selection

Alternatively, you could assign a certain number of stars corresponding to different photographers (e.g., if you are participating in a group project or had some of your participants making their own photographs). You could then combine all the images into an overall project file, and separate the images based on rank tags or colors simply as a means of identifying people or teams/groups involved in a project.

Secondary Analysis

If you take time to input the metadata and cross-reference your notes with your field notes, you have created the potential for powerful analysis. Revisiting data with new questions becomes easier, too. With well-developed metadata you can perform new searches on old images, video clips, or audio files that may not have been relevant in your previous round of inquiry. For example, in Crowder's work, research participant Donald regularly mentions his declining health and bouts with various hospitals and health care professionals. At the time, Crowder wrote about these comments in his field notes and in the metadata—as he took some photos of the piles of bills Donald collected over time (Figure 9.2), as well as his continual smoking habit. The purpose of the work was to investigate how residents over sixty-five years old in an underserved part of the city engaged with technology such as computers, the Internet, and cell phones.

After completing the research on technology and the elderly, Crowder returned to the data a year later to find discussions about health care and alternatives to bio-medicine in the neighborhood. Having relatively thorough notes, his basic searches on keywords like "health care," "biomedicine," and "physician relationships" turned up a variety of discussions and images that had not been part of his original focus. Just as importantly, organized field notes *correlated with images* allowed him to ask new questions of old data, such as (a) how do the elderly conceptualize their health and health care, (b) where do they turn for support, and (c) when are they most likely to seek health care. More central to Donald's situation, new questions concerning the quality of care he received while a patient in local hospitals and the

Figure 9.2 "Daily Stuff" (Donald's Medical Bills): As part of his research in East Houston with elderly residents, Crowder asked participants to photograph the things they liked about their lives and what they wanted to change. Donald took this image of the medical bills he received over the period of a few months, which his insurance was not going to pay. Courtesy of Donald. (Color original.)

EXPLORING IMAGES

subsequent turmoil he faced when having to pay his bills were all present in the data, but just never previously harvested.

New Information from Old Images

One of Crowder's ongoing exercises has been to revisit images he has made in El Alto, Bolivia since the early 1990s. Here his task is two-fold. First, he must select them carefully as he cannot afford the time (or storage space) to scan all of the images from before he went digital. Crowder begins with scanning images already selected for publications, presentations, or prints (for people). Next, Crowder considers other images that may hold more significance to him now than they did in the past, such as photos of people (who are now deceased) or of houses (that have since been expanded or the surrounding area changed significantly). Of course, being film, he scans the images at the highest resolution possible for archiving purposes, follows his naming conventions and provenance, creates JPEG files for everyday use, and then stores the TIFF files off-line. Once Crowder has the JPEG files, he must input the context so the images become useful research data.[6] Here is where his old field notes are exceptionally handy, as he can cut and paste the relevant notes directly into the metadata fields to identify people, places, and events. These are also valuable opportunities to *update* or *enhance* the ethnographic information by inputting new information and understandings regarding what has occurred since that photo was taken, such as if the person had passed away, been divorced, or moved out of town.

When Crowder sets time aside for scanning old images, he first establishes some type of limit (either time or number of images). Stopping at a designated place keeps scanning from becoming an all-afternoon process, and also makes it easy to know where to pick up later. For example, just scan fifteen photos and prepare them for metadata or spend two hours writing metadata, and that is all. Eventually, you will work your way through all of the images. Reread your field notes as you go to find information to transfer into the metadata fields. These data become usable immediately, as you can begin rethinking the meaning of the images. Since Crowder began this process, for instance, he has found portraits of people who have since passed away. These become invaluable when he returns to Bolivia and gives prints to family members who are often highly appreciative of the gesture.

Remember, this is an exercise—a process—and you must be patient with yourself and your field notes. As the authors have often experienced, revisiting notes and images often triggers memories and inspires rethinking previous research. Over time new patterns may appear, sometimes based on new knowledge, but often based on our own changing attitudes towards our work. Where the image may show us one thing early on, this may change as our perceptions mature enough that we become critical of why we took the photos and what we wrote about our participants.

With digital images (still or video) you will not lose time scanning them into your collection. Unlike film, you should not delete any from the collection, as you never know how they may benefit you later. To visualize your collection of images, it may be easiest to think about three concentric circles (Figure 9.3), the largest of which represents *all* of the images and is labeled appropriately. Even the worst images (except maybe those entirely out of focus or of your feet) are included in this group.[7] The next smallest circle includes a subset of all images that represents the *working* photos—those you deem potentially useful for publication, talks, photographic prints, and the like. Most exclusive, and in the smallest circle, are your "keepers/select"—those you consider the best for whatever reason and the ones you immediately look at when you need a descriptive photo of places, people, or events.[8]

Data Mining

Data mining, a term usually reserved for quantitative data, refers to revisiting old data with new questions to find new nuggets of information. As with both of our collections of images and field notes (Crowder's collection of Bolivia or Marion's collection of Ballroom), we argue that colleagues could search our database for just this purpose. The point is that libraries of photos can be mined if they are properly tagged and labeled to identify people, places, and events—and that such data mining provides access and information to researchers who may not otherwise have access.[9] The need for an application or program that combines the utility of image management and editing with the power of a text-driven database and analysis algorithm seems obvious to us. Unfortunately, while there are well-known qualitative data applications which allow the researcher to include images, audio files, and video in the synthesis of data (e.g., NVivo, HyperRESEARCH, ATLAS.ti) but not necessarily in the analysis itself.

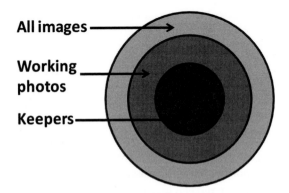

Figure 9.3 Organizational Levels.

EXPLORING IMAGES

Stephanie Takaragawa—Chapman University, United States

Being trained in the anthropology of visual communication, photographs have always been an intrinsic part of my work. While doing research for my dissertation on the role of the Japanese-American National Museum and its relationship to the construction of a Japanese-American collective identity, I took hundreds of photographs as sources of primary data to track the different exhibitions and changes that were made throughout their displays. These photographs were also used for photo elicitation purposes among museum curators, staff, and visitors to understand how they made meaning from these displays.

Photography had always been a hobby, even prior to my studies in anthropology, and I was used to developing my own negatives and printing my own images. I had initially assumed that the most important photographs would be documentation of the exhibitions that would largely be used to illustrate and support the argument that I was making in my writing and I strove for "typical" exhibition images, devoid of human context, for textual analysis. This wasn't always possible, because of activity in the museum, so many of my shots included visitors and employees of the museum that I could later crop out of the images. I chose to use digital images, rather than film simply because the process of collecting and organizing them made more sense and I was able to take many more photographs than I might have had I been using film because of the expense processing and developing images.

As often happens during research, my focus started to shift away from just exhibitions towards the audiences of the museum: how they were interacting with images, the demographics that visited the museum, and the role of museum staff. Off in a folder marked "random exhibition images" I had collected all of those images that weren't working for what I thought I wanted to study, but turned out to have all the data that I wanted and didn't even realize that I had.

Many sites host photo albums that allow users to store, display, and organize their images such as Picasa, MyPhotoAlbum, Shutterfly, Photobucket, Snapfish, and Flickr, but at the time, I stored them "old school" on my computer in files organized by date. As these types of sites become more widely-used the implications for preserving, organizing, and mining photographs for data become more accessible and available.

Programs for Exploring Images

Although we do not endorse any specific software package, free programs like Picasa are useful for helping you keep files organized and for performing basic or advanced searches. Something to keep in mind when employing an image database is that the application will want to *index* all of the images that you place in it (Adobe

Lightroom does this as well). *Indexing* means that the program will scan through all of the images you upload and place its own tags (or indices) on the files so it can recall them. In the case of Picasa, if you allow it to do so, the program will go through your entire computer and identify all of the photos on it. Some applications, like those that come with your digital camera, may do this when they automatically download the images from your camera—placing them in folders chronologically.[10]

Once the indexing is completed (which occurs each time you upload images into the program), you can search the images by date, time, and other metadata you provide. At the time of this printing, Apple and Google have introduced face recognition technology that will allow you to search your image database using facial features. In fact, Picasa will churn through your entire database and identify images of the same people, which you can then name for later use. Two caveats about using an image database like Picasa are that (a) you are downloading an application from the web that syncs with the Internet for various purposes (so your metadata may be transmitted), and (b) depending upon the size of your image files, indexing can take hours to complete.

You may ask yourself whether waiting for your computer to completely index the image files is necessary, and whether you want to depends on whether the application needs Internet access in order to properly perform. While Picasa may act as a sovereign application on your desktop (like Google Earth), if you do not connect to the Internet over a period of time, you may lose functionality with such web-based applications. Programs like Adobe Lightroom, on the other hand, do not depend upon the web for their functionality; they work offline just as well as when they're connected to the Internet. Although they may not have the functionality to upload images to webpages, they can still perform all basic functions, including searches. Remember, if using an online provider (e.g., Picasa), they may not be in business five years from now. What happens to your files, then?

Summary

In this chapter, we built upon the basics presented in Chapter 8, specifically the role of metadata and how to use them for future search and retrieval of images. More specifically, good metadata make the job of finding specific and applicable images all the easier. By inputting thorough metadata a researcher can use images for asking questions and conducting analysis, expanding the role of images beyond the simple illustration of text. We also discussed different search strategies for images, including chronological, ranking, and tagging. Furthermore, properly configured metadata allow researchers to revisit images with new questions, a technique we call secondary analysis. We ended the chapter with an introduction to various applications available for free and to purchase that help you further explore your photographs and videos.

We recommend that you begin with public domain applications or those bundled with your camera by the manufacturer and later move into more sophisticated for-pay applications if necessary.

Further Readings and Resources

- "Cataloging Images in Millennium: A Central Repository for Faculty-Owned Images" (Reilly and Singleton 2008)
- "Identifying and Interpreting Prewar and Wartime Jewish Photographs in Polish Digital Collections" (Sroka 2011)
- "Metadata" (Lange 2009)
- "Metadata and Digital Information" (Greenberg 2009)
- "News Photographers, Librarians, Tags, and Controlled Vocabularies: Balancing the Forces" (Neal 2008)
- "Semantic Metadata Interoperability in Digital Libraries" (Alemu 2011)

10

USING IMAGES

In this chapter you will learn about:

- A variety of ways to display and use images in your research work
- How to size your images for appropriate use
- Combining text with images

At this point we hope that you recognize the complexity of the issues surrounding the multiple types of digital files, including those for still and moving images, as well as audio and written documents. In this chapter we will discuss how researchers most commonly utilize their images to make their points or support the arguments they are presenting orally or in print. We have argued (and support) a position that prioritizes images as being as persuasive and meaningful as text for both academic and popular audiences. At the same time, we recognize that many (perhaps most) researchers will continue to supplement text with images. This chapter outlines how to prepare your images for presentations, publications, and the web no matter how you are using them.

Implementing Images In *Your* Work

Print

One of the best ways to continue making photos or videos with your research participants is to provide them copies of the work you create together. Small working prints are often an appreciated gift. They also provide something you can discuss with your participants (whether at the time or in subsequent fieldwork). *Photo-elicitation* is a method in which images (instead of a series of questions) are used to prompt a discussion. The images are used to elicit commentary, focus respondents' attention on a particular topic, or explore an interesting or puzzling aspect of what you are discovering. Part of the power of this method is that images frequently take conversations in directions that verbal questions alone cannot.[1] Be assured that you will not always know how participants will react to images (with pleasure, sadness, disinterest, or hostility). For Marion, for instance, feedback on images has helped in his understanding of what different people focus on and value in the aesthetics, performances, and techniques of ballroom dancing.

Besides making prints (for sharing or review with your participants), providing images for presentations (such as conference posters and presentations) and publications (such as journal articles and book chapters) is perhaps the single greatest use of still images in the social sciences. For each, you will need to select and edit with your audience in mind. Select photos that help you make your point rather than those that may be the prettiest. If it does not have anything to do with your topic, do not include it. Journal and book editors will provide specifics on the type of file they prefer (format, resolution), most commonly TIFF files at 300 dpi (see Table 10.1).[2]

Notes on Printing

Nearly all DSLRs today, as well as most higher end point-and-shoot cameras are capable of making both RAW or TIFF files along with smaller JPEG files. Remember, always make the largest size files possible, and only later use your

Table 10.1 Resolution and Printing (Megapixels vs. Maximum Print Size).

Megapixels v. Maximum Print Size				
Megapixels	Pixel Resolution	Print Size at 300 ppi	Print size at 200 ppi	Print size at 150 ppi
3	2048 x 1536	6.82" x 5.12"	10.24" x 7.68"	13.65" x 10.24"
4	2464 x 1632	8.21" x 5.44"	12.32" x 8.16"	16.42" x 10.88"
6	3008 x 2000	10.02" x 6.67"	15.04" x 10.00"	20.05" x 13.34"
8	3264 x 2448	10.88" x 8.16"	16.32" x 12.24"	21.76" x 16.32"
10	3872 x 2592	12.91" x 8.64"	19.36" x 12.96"	25.81" x 17.28"
12	4290 x 2800	14.30" x 9.34"	21.45" x 14.00"	28.60" x 18.67"
16	4920 x 3264	16.40" x 10.88"	24.60" x 16.32"	32.80" x 21.76"
21.1	5616 x 3744	18.72" x 12.48"	28.08" x 18.72"	37.44" x 24.96"
22.3	5760 x 3840	19.20" x 12.80"	28.80" x 19.20"	38.40" x 25.60"
35mm, scan	5380 x 3620	17.93" x 12.06"	26.90" x 18.10"	35.87" x 24.13"

Note: Dots per inch (dpi) refer to *printed* round dots on a page and the spaces between them. Pixels per inch (ppi) refer to square pixels as seen on a monitor, with no spaces between them. Pixel resolution varies from camera to camera. When you prepare a digital image for printing, you are essentially converting from pixels to dots, so 300 pixels become 150 dots and 150 spaces (i.e., 300 ppi to 150 dpi). As a general guide, this chart can help you determine the largest print size you should aim to produce given the resolution (megapixels) of your digital camera. Printed images made at 150 ppi will be pixelated and look blurry.

software to resize your selected images for printing. Once your files are resized for your preferred paper size, send the files to your personal printer or a professional lab. There is a significant quality difference between these, and while printing them yourself is relatively quick and inexpensive, these photos may not last long (perhaps less than five years) because the quality of the paper and ink is inferior to those at commercial labs.[3] Commercially made photos, on the other hand, may be viable without fading for up to ten years, depending upon the quality of the paper and the chemistry used.

Preparing Your Images

You can print your digital images in many different commercial places. Local drugstores and superstores are two commercial options that will accept your flash card. Or, you can upload your images to their online store for more convenience. More expensive professional labs can also help you with printing your images, and although it may take more time, the quality will be much higher. Chances are you may have your own color printer. In this case, the process of preparing your images is no different than below; however, your printer will need to be set up for using specific sizes and types of paper, so be sure to read your manual to attain the highest quality print. How you plan to use the images should help you decide how you want to print them.

- **Select** the images you want to print—use your photo manager to tag or rank the images.
- **Resize** the images and place in a different folder (named accordingly)—using the resize function. Be sure to select the size for 4 x 6" and *resolution* at 300 dpi. Depending upon the number of prints you select, the final image size and the speed of your computer, resizing twenty-five images may require less than three minutes.
- **Upload or export** the images to a flash drive, optical disc, or the website of the company who will print your photos. We like to keep older, smaller flash drives around, as 1–2 GB is plenty. These can be left at the lab or store until you retrieve the photos, or you can just take the flash drive to the store and upload the files to a machine there. Besides being safer for your images (e.g., in case you were to lose it), dedicating a flash drive just for this function means you do not compromise any data loss in case it becomes infected with a virus at the drugstore or lab.[4]

Digital Options

For researchers and academics, the most common use of images is as part of professional presentations. While Microsoft's PowerPoint tends to be the default application, there are alternatives such as OpenOffice's Impress and online applications such as Google Presentations or Prezi. Apple users have Keynote, although Microsoft provides a PowerPoint version for Apple computers. There also are endless Linux freeware presentation applications. Here are some suggestions to help you make stronger image-based presentations:

- Use dark backgrounds, such as black, dark gray, dark blue, or a dark maroon with light gray text.
- Size your images to fit the space. The default size for PowerPoint workspace is 10 x 7.5", and as we have stated earlier, you only need 72 dpi for digital projection.
- Keep any transitions simple (e.g., fade or dissolve).
- Select "fade through black" for any animations to provide a slideshow appearance.
- Center your images.
- If you must place text over your image, make sure the font, size, and color are legible. A sans serif font like Arial or Century Gothic works well, and a slightly gray color font trumps white.
- Include the minimum amount of text needed as you want your viewers to engage with you rather than just sit there reading.

One alternative to printing photos (whether for yourself or participants) is the **digital frame**—a small electronic screen that accepts memory cards to augment its onboard memory, in which you can store many photos.[5] Simple software runs the frame, allowing the user to cycle through loaded images, play music, and watch small video files. Digital frames range in size and price, depending upon quality of the screen, software, size, and brand. While significantly more expensive than the standard photo album, digital photo frames allow you to do a number of things you cannot without them. First and foremost, they can hold thousands of images for review without the need of a computer, allowing those who are computer illiterate to enjoy the images without the hassle of a computer. Price, portability, and ease of use make these excellent gifts for participants who do not own or operate a computer. Second, digital photo frames are solid state (have no moving parts) and can potentially last longer than prints.

Here is an example of a useful application with the digital frame. We had scanned photographs from a participant's personal collection/archive that she discussed over the course of several interviews. She allowed us to scan the images in her home and when we returned we gave her a digital frame with all of the scanned images loaded on it (and other digital ones from the project, too). Since she is elderly and not computer literate, the frame allowed her the opportunity to enjoy old images more regularly. Also, realize that digital frames may create more buy-in with the participants—which can help build rapport and trust for the on-going and/or larger visual projects in the future. Finally, if you give a digital frame to anyone, be sure to preload the images and discuss the instructions for using the frame before leaving.

Digital storytelling is a method for taking your photos (and videos) and sequencing them with an audio track to create a short (typically three to five minute) video that tells a story. Using applications like iMovie or Final Cut Pro on Apple computers, or Microsoft Moviemaker or Adobe Premier for Windows-based computers allows you to order your images in such a way that they tell a story. Having students make digital stories is an excellent exercise as it requires them to integrate their images with research and edit them all down to something that must make a point in a short period of time. For professionals, digital stories are an excellent means for discussing research and placing it on a website, so people can see what you do or learn more about an aspect of your work. See the resources listed at the end of this chapter for more about digital storytelling, as it has become a very popular and elegant means for integrating still images with audio and voice to create effective pieces of visual work.

Unlike the other digital image processes we have discussed, when preparing your images to use in digital stories they cannot be 72 dpi. Rather, you must use a significantly higher resolution, almost as if you were making them print size. Keeping images large is key; because the digital story will be compressed and reformatted into video files, like WAV or MP4, maximizing the amount of information in each image is paramount to your images looking good in a digital story. By mentioning compression and reformatting, we want to draw your attention to a very important logistical matter: You need to be sure that your video can actually be viewed on your own computer as well as on others. This is where codecs are key.

Codecs are computer applications that compress-decompress (or, more colloquially, encode-decode) data. They encode for storage, encryption, or transmission and then decode for playback or retrieval. Various devices accomplish this in a number of ways and typically require you to install the appropriate codec[6] on your computer in order to play the signal itself. Compression essentially aims to preserve the integrity of the file while removing unnecessary data from the file (although there are lossless codecs). There is no single best codec for video or audio; rather, it depends upon how you intend to use the compressed data. While compressed MP3 audio files are compressed and MP4 video files are perhaps the most common in use today, make sure that your computer has the appropriate codecs installed to read the data from your video camera and microphones.

Considerations for Posting Images Online

A few things to keep in mind before posting your research images on the Internet:

- To what end are these images serving you by placing them on the web?
  - Are you placing them online because you are being followed by family and friends and want them to know what you are working on, or is the blog part of the research itself?

- Are you looking for feedback from colleagues (and the world) about your research questions, methods, and data?
- How will you secure your images?
  - Can you restrict access to the images so they are not public?
  - Can they be traced back to you?
- Do you have consent from those appearing in the image?
- Will you include text with the images? If so, why?
- Do you plan to remove the images from the web at any time in the future?
- Have you properly sized your images for electronic use?
  - Is a watermark appropriate? Remember, if you do not want the images distributed, do not place them on the web.

Images and Text

Because images rarely stand alone, you will want, and will probably be expected, to provide text to accompany them. When thinking about the appropriate text, consider your audience and remember our earlier discussion concerning the differences between *content* and *context*. Do you need to explain what is taking place in the image, or do you need to discuss the environment in which the image was made? Or, a combination of the two? If providing a caption, you may simply need to identify the subject, place, and year. However, a more involved description may better complement an article or installation. If so, will your audience have the time or patience to read everything you think you need to discuss? Perhaps the most difficult aspect of writing for an image is effectively balancing the text and the image. Always keep in mind that as researchers we probably know much more about the subjects than our readers may need or want to know. As such, our task is to strike a balance between (a) what we feel is necessary in order to make our point without (b) overburdening the reader with superfluous information (i.e., so much that it detracts from the intent of the image itself). When writing for images we recommend the following:

- Keep your text to a minimum (what this is depends upon the medium).
  - For posters and PowerPoint presentations, remember that you can speak to the images themselves, so the absolute minimum is required.
  - For publications, such as journal articles or webpages, you must consider your audience and what is expected of authors. For text specifically considering the context of an image, no more than five sentences and preferably three.
- Write concisely and stress context over content. Viewers can often discern what is going on, what they need to know is why or how it is taking place or is significant.
- Save technical details, unless requested by the editor, for endnotes. Camera make and model, lens, aperture, and speed are each interesting bits of data, but not appropriate for all audiences.

Know that the marriage of text and image is a matter of philosophical discussion regularly visited in art circles as well as within academic enclaves, with some individuals asserting very strong points of view on this topic. The spectrum of such views appears in Internet chat rooms, blogs, and webpages. In the end, you must be respectful of your own work and the people with whom you work. That being said, be open to editors and colleagues helping you meld your prose with your images, since they—as readers—will see the effective combination of the two quite differently than you. Availing yourself of the perspectives of others' eyes and ears is often quite useful and educational.

SEEING AND SHOWING TOURISM

Jenny Chio—Emory University, United States

While sightseeing is an engrained feature of tourism experience for *tourists*, the experience of being seen as a "sight" is equally mundane for individuals and communities working in tourism destinations.[7] Indeed, tourism is very much about looking as a physical and psychological act. The relationships between tourism, media representations, photographic practices, cultural performances, and even the built environment (e.g., iconic buildings such as the Sydney Opera House) suggest theoretically innovative and challenging approaches to the use and study of images in tourism studies research.

To analyze what residents of two rural, ethnic minority tourism villages in southwestern China thought about tourism development in their communities, during my ethnographic fieldwork I began sharing clips of my own video recordings with village residents. This methodology emerged at the request of the community; my initial intention had been to shoot footage for an ethnographic film while conducting fieldwork. However, as village residents saw me recording their daily activities and asking questions about the day-to-day preparations involved in catering to tourists, a few local individuals began asking to see the recordings. I reciprocated by creating short films from my footage, incorporating scenic clips and interviews from both villages into a ten to twenty minute long video that I would burn onto video compact discs (VCDs, the most common format played in the villages). I showed these videos to families and individuals in each village, and I video recorded the viewings and discussions between myself and the audience.

By sharing my own videos with local residents, I realized quickly that instead of just studying how tourism interacted with visual practices *for* tourists, I was beginning to understand how the visual world was put to work in the lives of the toured. When viewing my short edited films, residents of each village both consumed images (of themselves and of the other village), and they became potential image producers as they enumerated to me which scenes they found attractive, beautiful, good for tourism, and so forth. Individuals would also make suggestions to me about what I should film

Figure 10.1 Screening Video: TOP: A child recognizes her family in the video in upper Jidao village. BOTTOM: Villagers putting on a video to watch in upper Jidao village. ©2006 Jenny Chio. (Film frames.)

next in order to best represent their villages as tourism destinations. This visual research method, of seeing and showing videos during fieldwork, thus allowed me to begin to unravel how village residents literally saw tourism developments in their village; and, by extension, how they viewed the prospects and perils of these changes on community relationships, the local environment, and everyday livelihoods.

Summary

This chapter drew on insights and advice from previous chapters to help you think about how to implement images in your own work, and then how to do so. Historically, images have been most commonly used in print media; we discussed how to prepare them—whether for use in the field or as part of journal submissions. Because digital displays (e.g., digital photo frames, PowerPoint presentations) require smaller files (less information), we next outlined some basic parameters for formatting to digital outputs. Finally, we suggested key issues to consider when combining text with images, and how to evaluate an appropriate balance.

Further Readings and Resources

- *The Focal Encyclopedia of Photography: Digital Imaging, Theory and Applications, History and Science* (Peres 2007)
- "Designing with Mobile Digital Storytelling in Rural Africa" (Bidwell et al. 2010)
- "Digital Storytelling: A Powerful Technology Tool for the 21st Century Classroom" (Robin 2008)
- "Digital Storytelling as a Signature Pedagogy for the New Humanities" (Benmayor 2008)
- "Making Things Our Own: The Indigenous Aesthetic in Digital Storytelling" (Hopkins 2006)
- "How Do People Manage Their Digital Photographs?" (Rodden and Wood 2003)
- "In Poor Light" (Smith 2010)

CONCLUSION

In the first section of this book, Image Basics, we introduced the foundational topics of visual ethics, thinking visually, and thinking of images as data. In all honesty, this is the most important section of the book, as these concepts are the foundation for all visual research. The next section, Making Images, started with an overview of the history of cameras in social science research, and then introduced technical and production issues associated with photography, video, and multimedia for social research. The concluding section, Using Images, considered what to do with your images (still and moving), and highlighted organization, storage, archiving, doing research from your images, and using images to present your work (both to research participants and professional audiences).

Showing What You Mean

Given the amount of human neural capacity dedicated to visual information, visuals can be powerful tools.[1] That said, visuals are a *method* of research and presentation, and poorly used when utilized from a one-size-fits-all approach. Just as there is no such thing as the best research method (only better matches between question and method), there is no such thing as the best visual research or presentation strategy. Visual materials and modalities should be chosen for specific communicative aims, and never simply for the sake of using visuals.

Matching Method to Message

Matching method to message requires asking a few key questions. First, what is the thrust of the material being presented? Is it about behavior, architecture, land use, or artifacts? Or is it about subjective experience or individual narrative? Any one of these topics might make good use of visuals, but not the same ones. Looking at behavior as an example: what behavior is being addressed, and to what ends? A video clip panning across a landscape is more useful in some situations while a map of the same landscape would be more appropriate in others. But what if the points being discussed concern indigenous persons' feelings about their traditional lands? Perhaps visual materials help orient an unfamiliar audience, or allow the research participants to speak for themselves. Conversely, however, the same visuals may ultimately serve more as distractions rather than allowing the focus to remain on the feelings of those being discussed. In such a case the choice *not* to use visuals (or at least not to do so in conjunction with that part of the project) may well be the best decision.

General Guidelines

Following these simple guidelines can provide clearer use and more direct presentation of visual materials, thereby facilitating your efforts to effectively show what you mean:

- *Do not use visuals for their own sake.* Does a photograph, a chart, an illustration, a map, or a video clip best reveal (as part of your research) the issues you are assessing? Does the visual best represent, as part of your presentations, the understandings you have gained? Use whichever one(s) do this best, and if none add to your message, do not use anything! Whatever doesn't help make the point distracts from it.
- *Less is more.* While three bulleted titles draw attention to key themes, a full screen of text does not. Likewise, a variety of animations, wipes, and fades typically distract—and hence detract—from content, and only rarely augment an underlying point.
- *Know your audience.* You need to know with whom you are trying to communicate in order to decide the best means of presenting your materials. Think about this at every step of the process (planning, in the field, and while preparing your finished materials).
- *Use the tools.* Too many presentations use colorful backgrounds with embedded patterns and graphics in an effort to present a more finished look. To the contrary however, pertinent materials often become nearly impossible to discern amidst superfluous backgrounds, colors, and graphics.
  - o Simple, solid-color backgrounds are often best. Likewise, lighter colored text on a dark background is easier to read than dark text on a light background.[2]
  - o Evaluate what will actually be seen. What appears well on a laptop screen doesn't always translate well to projected imagery, in a printed book, or as part of a display—so evaluate your materials as they will be presented.
- *It takes time.* However long you spend creating visual data, plan to spend at least twice as long reviewing, sorting, selecting, and editing. After all, what is the point of having the data if you do not take the time to assess it and use it?

Thinking Visually in the Field

The key to good research is finding a way to investigate something and then having a way to make sense of whatever you find. This is the same for visual research. Where visual research differs—and as the materials in this book have been discussing—is in how imagery represents reality. The guidelines above are just that, guidelines. They are not rules. There is no right way to do visual research after all (which does not mean there are not lots of wrong ways, such as those that ignore important ethical considerations). Just to show you what we mean, go back and skim through the case studies featured in each chapter of this book. As you can see, the issues and topics introduced in this text can be applied—and are equally valuable—across vastly different fieldwork scenarios. So what should you take away from this book? This is not a summary or a step list for how to do visual research. Rather, we have provided you with a new, broader, and more nuanced way of thinking visually.

Further Readings and Resources

- *Doing Visual Research* (Mitchell 2011)
- *Viewpoints: Visual Anthropologists at Work* (Strong and Wilder 2009)
- *Visual Research Methods in the Social Sciences: Awakening Visions* (Spencer 2011)

APPENDIX I: GLOSSARY

Angle   See perspective

Aperture   The adjustable opening in a camera lens that determines how *much* light reaches the sensor (per unit time)

B-roll   Supplemental footage used to add context and meaning to a sequence

Bandwidth   Rate of data transfer, also known as throughput or bit rate, usually in bits per second (bps)

Composition   The arrangement of objects within an image (within the framing)

Crop   To define new limits for an image

Dark storage   One type of archiving that involves saving data to a hard drive that is then turned off until the data are needed for retrieval

Depth of field (DOF)   Zone of acceptable sharpness both in front of and behind the main focus point

Exposure/exposure value (EV)   The amount of light received by the camera sensor (or film)

F-stop   See aperture

Framing   What shows up within the image

Image resolution   The number of pixels in an image

Informed consent   Participants uncoerced willingness to participate in projects they fully understand (including the right to withdraw approval at any time)

ISO setting   The sensor's sensitivity to light

Lens speed   Maximum aperture of a lens

Lighting   The amount, source, and location of light sources in an image

Mise-en-scène   The spatial organization of the frame

Normal (perspective/lens)   A perspective approximating that of the human eye

Prime lens   Any lens with a fixed focal length (i.e., cannot zoom)

Perspective   The position of the camera relative to the subject (e.g., straight on, from the side, eye level, below, or above the subject, etc.)

Photo-elicitation   Using photos or images to trigger responses and feedback; also, image-elecitation

Reformatting   Converting a digital image from one file type to another

Sensitivity   see ISO setting

Shutter speed   How long a camera sensor is exposed to light

Telephoto   A narrower perspective than the field of vision of the human eye

Thumbnail   Reduced size image that is a facsimile of the original but smaller

Timestamp   Sequence of characters denoting when something occurred, such as saving a file or making an image (e.g., date and time)

Visual ethics   The ethical concerns of working with and using visual images

Visual literacy   Competence in discerning and interpreting visual experiences and encounters, including actions and objects, that is fundamental to visual learning and communication (coined by John Debes in 1969); for more see the International Visual Literacy Association (http://www.ivla.org)

White balance   Camera and display setting used to make sure that whites look white that accounts for color casts of different light wavelengths

Wide angle   A wider perspective than the field of vision of the human eye

Workflow   Sequential steps to achieve a specific outcome and each step is necessary before moving to the following step, resulting in the idea of a flow

APPENDIX II: ONLINE RESOURCES

Chapter 1

- American Anthropological Association Ethics Resources
  - www.aaanet.org/cmtes/ethics/Ethics-Resources.cfm

Chapter 2

- International Visual Literacy Association
  - www.ivla.org
- Periodic Table of Visualization Methods (geared toward Communication, Engineering, and Business disciplines)
  - www.visual-literacy.org/periodic_table/periodic_table.html
- The Associated Press Statement of News Values and Principles
  - www.ap.org/company/news-values

Chapter 3

- The Donald A. Cadzow Photograph Collection (Smithsonian Collections Blog)
  - www.si-siris.blogspot.com/2012/01/donald-cadzow-photograph-collection.html

Chapter 4

- International Visual Sociology Association
  - www.visualsociology.org
- News and Resources for Visual Anthropology
  - www.visualanthropology.net/
- Society for Visual Anthropology
  - societyforvisualanthropology.org

Chapter 5

- CameraSim: DSLR Photography Demystified
  - camerasim.com/
- Digital Photography Review (helpful equipment reviews and educational articles)
  - www.dpreview.com/

Chapter 6

- Online resources for production and post-production techniques and instruction
  - www.lynda.com
  - www.shootsmarter.com

Chapter 7

- Free blogging sites
  - www.blogger.com
  - wordpress.com
- Instruction for webpages and multimedia
  - www.shortcourses.com
  - www.w3schools.com
- Instruction for putting it all together in multimedia
  - www.storycenter.org
  - animoto.com

Chapter 8

- Applications for photo editing and management
  - Free photo editing applications: IrfanView, PhotoScape, GIMP, Paint.NET, Pixlr, Photo Pos Pro, FotoFlexer
  - Software included with operating systems: Windows Live Photo Gallery, Apple iPhoto, Google Picasa
  - Paid software: Adobe Photoshop, ACDSee, Photodex, Paintshop Photo Pro
- Easy to use monitor dpi/ppi (dots per inch/pixels per inch) calculator
  - members.ping.de/~sven/dpi.html
- Backup and sync applications
  - DeepBurner, Autobackup 3.0, SynchBackSE, ComparatorPro, DirSync Pro (open source)
- Photoshop Basics: Color Balance
  - https://www.youtube.com/watch?v=w_Ws9amshi0
- Best Practices for File-Naming
  - www.records.ncdcr.gov/erecords/filenaming_20080508_final.pdf
- Guidelines on File Naming Conventions for Digital Collections
  - ucblibraries.colorado.edu/systems/digitalinitiatives/docs/filename guidelines.pdf
- Archive formats by the United States Library of Congress
  - www.digitalpreservation.gov/formats

Chapter 9

- Dublin Core Metadata Initiative
  - www.dublincore.org/
- Human Relation Area Files (eHRAF World Cultures)
  - www.yale.edu/hraf/

Chapter 10

- Lucid Chart (for help making your own flow charts and diagrams)
  - https://www.lucidchart.com
- The Center for Digital Storytelling
  - www.storycenter.org
- Speed Test (for testing your internet connection's upload and download speeds)
  - www.speedtest.net
    - Remember, having sufficient speed in both directions will allow you to most effectively and efficiently place your images online
- Luminous Landscape (for finding articles, tutorials, product reviews, and photos)
  - www.luminous-landscape.com
    - Comprehensive site dedicated to documentary, landscape, and nature photography

NOTES

Introduction

1. Between us we have designed and taught undergraduate and graduate courses in visual anthropology, visual studies, and contemporary ethnographic film, pre-screened and juried the 2009–2012 Society for Visual Anthropology Film and Media Festivals. We have taught the two-part "Photography for the Field" workshops at the 2008–2012 American Anthropological Association (AAA) national meetings and the 2008, 2009, 2012, and (online) 2013 National Science Foundation (NSF)-sponsored Short Course in Research Methods "Systematic Techniques For Gathering And Analyzing Visual Data." We have also organized the Digital Image Display at the 2009–2011 AAA national meetings.

2. Jenny Chio was at the University of Sydney (Australia) when she contributed her case study for Chapter 10.

1 The Ethics of Images

1. See Perry and Marion (2010) for an overview of visual ethics in anthropology and allied disciplines.

2. For example, think of the use, dissemination, and circulation of personal images through social networking (e.g., Facebook, Twitter).

3. See Lutz and Collins (1993) for a critique of many earlier examples of such work.

4. See Marion (2011) for a more comprehensive discussion of the ethical considerations involved in preparing the images for Ericksen (2011).

2 The Basics of Thinking Visually

1. This is Freeman's point in noting, "photographs are ambiguous. They may be worth a thousand words, but it can be any thousand words" (2009: 61).

2. In these ways documentary photography is more related to ethnographic imagery.

3. For an academic critique of *National Geographic*, see Lutz and Collins (1993).

4. For example, compare the reviews by Roberts (2000) and Viditz-Ward (2000) regarding a book made by Western photographers on African ceremonies to see how controversial and "lacking" these reviews feel the photographers got it.

5. For various perspectives on anthropology and art see *Anthropologies of Art* (Westermann 2005), *Between Art and Anthropology: Contemporary Ethnographic Practice* and *Contemporary Art and Anthropology* (Schneider and Wright 2006a, 2006b), *Anthropology, Art and Cultural Production: Histories, Themes, Perspectives* (Svasek 2007), and *Community Art: An Anthropological Perspective* (Crehan 2011).

6. For a recent overview of the history of visual anthropology, see the edited volume *Made to Be Seen: Perspectives on the History of Visual Anthropology* (Banks and Ruby 2011); also see Engelbrecht (2007), Heider (2006, Chapter 2), and Rose (2007).

7. See, for example, *Photographic Composition: A Visual Guide* by Zakia and Page (2011).

8. Over 25 years ago John Collier, Jr. and Malcolm Collier made a similar point for ethnographic film, noting that "artistry is only a means, for the end is cultural authenticity" (1986: 158).

9. Aesthetics are certainly considered by some to be cultural, although it is argued that there is an innate biophysical recognition of what is pleasing to the eye (e.g., the rule of thirds as discussed in Chapter 5).

10. This includes the audience's assumptions about the images and the participants/subjects, before ever viewing the images.

11. First used by Strand (1917), see Nickel (2001) for more on previsioning in photography. For a related use of the concept, see Sterritt (2000).

12. Quickly becoming one of Marion's signature images, this picture circulated online, appeared in *Dance Beat* in the United States, *Dance News* in the United Kingdom, and on the website of DecaDance Photography (for whom Marion occasionally works as a guest photographer). It has provided a powerful illustration in various professional talks and academic publications (e.g., Marion 2008: 41, Marion 2010: 26).

3 Thinking of Images as Data

1. For example, Dowdall and Gordon (1989) use photographs as data for their historical sociological analysis of mental hospitals. They identify appraisal, inquiry, and interpretation as three levels of working with images as data.

2. This formulation is based on ideas posited by David MacDougal (2006: 1–4).

3. For more on the life of Alice Cunningham Fletcher, see Scherer and DeMallie (2013).

4. For more information see www.nmnh.si.edu/naa/kiowa/mooney.htm.

5. Such considerations of scale are equally applicable to research concerning material culture, archaeology, and related fields where having an image of the object in question (whole), specific features (narrow), and the wider context of the object (broad) are all important perspectives that gain value when considered in conjunction.

6. For an interesting and related understanding of still imagery, see Bourdieu (2012) that links his writing to 130 of the photographs he took while serving in Algeria in the French army.

7. For a concise overview of the method in anthropology and sociology, see Harper (2002).

4 Cameras in Social Science Research

1. The resources listed at the end of this chapter include texts discussing the history of photography and film in research.

2. The *camera obscura* and pinhole cameras date back as far as the fourth century B.C.E., when these were used for drawing images.

3. As Jacknis (personal communication 2012) points out, "professional photographers... knew how to take a good picture, while anthropologists many times made crummy pictures because they didn't understand the technology."

4. Williams was Oxford-trained and a student of Malinowski, also known for his deft use of a camera.

5. See, for example, Harper (1988), Edwards (1994), Heider (2006), and Durington and Ruby (2011).

6. Visual sociology and visual anthropology differ historically on the role images play in their methods and analyses, with sociology historically emphasizing issues of validity, sampling, and purpose.

7. This can have cascading effects for the researcher and the data throughout their fieldwork (e.g., Marion 2010).

8. Additional obstacles came from lack of postproduction know-how and postproduction costs.

9. Perhaps the most famous examples of such staging are the outdoor performance of temple ceremonies in *Trance and Dance in Bali* by Bateson and Mead (1952), as well as the double-sized half igloo used in filming Flaherty's *Nanook of the North* (1922).

10. On the downside, many such efforts involve no background or training regarding visual research.

11. See Hammond (2004) for a discussion of how the reflexive use of imagery responds to the critique of the theoretical turn.

5 Photography

1. Just a quick note on zoom lenses: A lens marked 28–100mm f/3.5–5.6 means that it has a maximum aperture of f/3.5 when zoomed out to 28mm and a maximum aperture of f/5.6 when zoomed in to 100mm. While there are zoom lenses that have a constant maximum aperture, these are much more expensive, professionally targeted lenses. For our purposes, then, it is important that you consider the maximum aperture of a lens *at the focal length you intend to use it*.

2. This is really all that is going on with aperture settings; it just looks more complicated because to halve the aperture *surface*—and thus the light allowed—the *diameter* of the aperture reduces by a factor of 1.4 (the square root of two). So now you know and understand why f/4 allows through double the light of f/5.6.

3. If you plan to make videos on the same camera, however, realize that high definition video requires high write speeds and that SD cards are rated by class (anything above Class 6 should suffice for on-board video).

4. Different companies have proprietary types of RAW files, which often require special plug-ins to open, so check the specifics for each manufacturer.

5. SLR = Single Lens Reflex; DSLR = Digital Single Lens Reflex.

6. A closely related issue concerns calibrating your camera to account for the color casts of different wavelengths of light. In photography and videography, this is known as **white balance** (WB). Some adjustments can be made after the fact (via software), but you should carefully read your camera's instructions for setting WB, and remember to reset this every time you the light changes (such as when you switch locations, angles or as sunlight comes and goes).

7. Some cameras provide grid lines as options in their viewfinders or on their rear screens. Use them if possible.

6 Video

1. Do not forget, however, that video is not a substitute for observation and note-taking. Indeed, reviewing your footage requires at least as much attention for you to unpack the content of your footage.

2. This assumes you are dealing with populations where written and signed consents are viable. In absolutely every case, however, you should have a record of consent, such as that given on video.

149

3. From Cartwright and Romero (2009).

4. Jean Rouche, for instance, perfected that *cinéma vérité* feel in his work, but entire films were not shot from his shoulder. You may also want to consider counterbalancing technologies (e.g., a Steadicam system) that allow you to walk with a video camera, but these are significantly more expensive and require practice to use effectively. Shortcuts for building your own stabilizing system (e.g., a backpack with weights and straps) can be found on a variety of web pages, so if relevant to your work, (a) do some research and (b) practice.

5. As a rule of thumb, do not zoom while filming. Instead, stop, zoom, and then begin recording again.

6. The term B-roll derives from linear-based editing in which supplementary footage was placed on the B (i.e., A and B) deck.

7. A transducer is a device that converts one form of energy to another which, in a microphone, generally involves converting acoustic energy (air pressure) to electrical signals. Types of transducers vary within microphones, from ribbons (like an ear drum) or moving coils (like a loudspeaker) to the changing of electrical charge between metal plates (condenser). Each type has advantages and disadvantages as far as sensitivity and durability.

8. For more sophisticated set-ups, a small field mixer allows you to mix multiple microphones on the left, right and/or center channels, before being recorded on the soundtrack which you can also monitor with headphones.

9. The silver lining to this situation was that when needing to re-film, these students already knew which angles and shots they felt would help them best tell the roller derby story. In other words, familiarity with the setting helped them prevision (Chapter 2) the images and sequences they wanted to record.

10. Almost all modern digital point-and-shoot and DSLR cameras offer a video capture feature, although not all are high-definition quality. These, too, will satisfy the exercise.

7 Multimedia

1. Technically video is multimedia (as is a photo with captioning), but in this chapter we are addressing multimedia as it is most commonly conceived; that is, not just for production, but also for evaluation and presentation.

2. See Pink (2011) regarding the potentials and challenges of digital visual anthropology.

3. Always check with organizations to find out their expectations regarding sizes, colors, and layout design, as well as any sample templates that may be available.

4. Mobile phones, e-book readers, tablet computers, and other locative media provide another layer of expansion.

5. Both blogs and webpages can be shared via Facebook and Twitter (among others)—which can then get reposted by people who have never seen your site itself—and viewers can request RSS (Really Simple Syndication) feeds to receive e-mails alerting them to site or post updates.

6. Online web instruction is a great source for learning the basics, which you can develop further through professionally-led workshops.

7. For another good example, see *Maring Interactive* by Allison and Marek Jablonko at jablonko-maring.pacific-credo.fr.

8. See Levy et al. (2001), Levy and Smith (2007), Levy et al. (2010), and Petrovic et al. (2011).

9. *Dane Wajich—Dane-zaa Stories and Songs: Dreamers and the Land* was produced in collaboration with Amber Ridington and the Doig River First Nation. It can be accessed at http://www.virtualmuseum.ca/Exhibitions/Danewajich.

10. *Inuvialuit Living History* is a production of the Inuvialuit Cultural Resource Center, and was produced in collaboration with Natasha Lyons, Catherine Cockney, Charles Arnold, Mervin Joe, Albert Elias, Stephen Loring, and Culture Code. It can be accessed at http://www.inuvialuitlivinghistory.ca.

11. For some of the work that *is* being done regarding online and virtual research, see Boellstroff (2008), Hine (2000, 2005), Kozinets (2009), and Miller and Slater (2001).

8 Storage and Organization

1. Because audiences differ, the conventions we suggest for presentations and social science research are not the same as those promoted or endorsed by information science or professional archivists. Different groups have different needs, knowledge, expectations, and understandings.

2. Using lower case filenames makes it considerably easier to tell the difference between a lower case letter o and a zero.

3. It's fine if you prefer the filmstrip or loupe mode, as each provides a specific means for engaging with the images.

4. See below regarding tagging and ranking images. These terrific features help track your previous thinking whenever you revisit your images.

5. Over time which image you keep in your "keepers" or "select" folder may change. That is understandable, and another reason why the images in this folder are copied from files you still have elsewhere.

6. Newer devices and programs can usually determine when images need to be rotated for proper viewing (i.e., so a vertical photo doesn't appear horizontally). The spatial orientation of data from the camera (when the photo was taken) may be lost when resizing images, however, so be ready to rotate images manually.

7. This is a good time to use the <shift-click> or <control-click> actions to highlight multiple images, so the metadata you type into the fields will be applied to all of the highlighted images.

8. When making electronic slideshows, only use images sized to 72 ppi. Sometimes presenters mistakenly use full-size images in their presentations, creating huge (over 200 MB) rather than equally resolved slides at smaller file sizes.

9. While there is a growing trend to share images via the cloud, most people will continue attaching image files to emails and large files will quickly (and frustratingly) fill up recipients' inboxes.

10. Beyond facilitating ease of use, optimizing and resizing your images provides a small level of security. Downsampling your images to no higher than 72 dpi will ensure that while they're easily viewable on the web, they are not resolved enough for others to download and print against your wishes.

11. Purists may argue that all images should be kept in one large file (without subfiles) and that you should use the database in order to cull through your images to find the ones you need at the time and then export those files for use. Experience has taught us that sometimes it is just easier to keep images of a certain type in their own folder (even when duplicating images). But this is exactly why keeping your files properly named and separated is paramount—that way you can grab and go, knowing exactly what you have. Today storage is so inexpensive that keeping multiple copies of different sized photos is not problematic.

12. In fact, you can create a photo album in PowerPoint and that will automatically bring the images into the program, placing each image on its own slide. You can then manipulate the backgrounds and animations once there.

---

13. Sometimes computers will time-out while uploading large files because the computer doesn't receive input from the keyboard.

14. It is the interface connecting external drives to your computer that sets the speed limit to read and write files, not the media itself (which typically has much faster read and write times).

15. USB 3.0 interfaces are backwards compatible and will still read USB 2.0 drives.

16. As previously noted cloud storage is viable, but will be limited by your Internet speed (so uploads and downloads could possibly take some time depending upon the bandwidth available). If you are affiliated with a university, check with their information technology group to see how much online storage they offer students, faculty, and staff and how to access it. Also note that Amazon, Apple, and Google offer popular cloud storage options, some for free and offering more storage for a price.

17. Now verging on the pricey 128 GB of storage, it is possible to store your work on solid-state media (no moving parts) that require very little physical space (your pocket or keychain).

18. Because of constant technological progress, it is hard to predict the best methods and formats to archive your materials. Our suggestion is to archive formats that are either open source or industry standards. See the suggested resources at the end of the chapter. Today, there are a variety of options for archiving your data, each of which requires redundancy. One photographer writes that he stores all of his images on Gold Mitsui CDs and DVDs, which he places in jewel cases, and then prints thumbnails on a card for the cover so that within minutes he can find his files (Brooks 2011). We do not recommend this form of archiving digital data, as even these Gold optical discs will lose data over time.

9 Exploring Images

1. These are called header files, and if you want to know more about their unique characteristics, search for EXIF or exchangeable image file format.

2. Effectively, now Crowder has three copies of the file. He can erase the audio file on the recorder once he input all of his notes and copies that over the earlier version on the hard drive.

3. This is an excellent means for cross referencing your field notes with the metadata in your files—especially if you identify that the notes are the same for a specific recording.

4. Audacity is an open source, cross platform sound recorder and editor. It is free and works on Windows and Apple platforms.

5. Make sure that the date and time on your camera is set correctly, so when the metadata are placed, they are accurate (especially if you regularly travel between time zones). To be safe, check your time zone every time you change batteries.

6. Crowder worries more about the IPTC metadata than the EXIF-like descriptors of the image, although he will include the film type and speed and possibly the camera he used if he remembers those specifics.

7. One argument for keeping all images may not have to deal with the photo itself, but possibly the metadata it provides. For example, perhaps the time and date stamp may be useful in locating a situation or moment when something happened. Like a cash register receipt, you may remember you took the photo, but not when. This time stamp will help establish that moment for the record.

8. Remember you can name these anything that makes sense to you, for example, Reilly states that in her digital library these same groups and circles are respectively named Preservation, Access, and Collection.

9. Note: This is beginning to sound like the HRAF's standardized codes that allow general users to locate materials and make comparisons.

10. Because these tags are based on the EXIF information, if your camera's clock and calendar are incorrectly set your organization could be jeopardized. Be especially careful about this when you are travelling between different time zones (a lesson Marion learned the hard way shooting at ballroom competitions across the United States, Canada, and Europe).

10 Using Images

1. For a concise overview of the method in anthropology and sociology, see Harper (2002).

2. They may ask for images to be sized in pixels per inch (versus dots per inch), so find out what is required before you submit.

3. All images fade, and based upon the light they're exposed to over time you will see a noticeable shift to the longer wavelengths (reds). Ink jet and dye prints made on home-based printers can only claim to be archival, but time has not yet shown how long these can be expected to last.

4. Despite what you may think, public use computers are not safe and can easily transfer viruses to your flash drive, which you may not realize until you bring it home and infect your system. Always run virus protection and malware detection software on your flash drives after you leave them anywhere.

5. Photos for the frames can be batch resized down to the exact dimensions of the frame at 72 dots per inch, making these image files quite small, so thousands of decently resolved images can be placed on a small card or on the frame itself.

6. Standard codecs exist for both audio and video; however, some companies may develop proprietary codecs for protection as well as transmission purposes.

7. For a longer discussion of this research methodology, see Chio (2011).

Conclusion

1. The sections "Showing What You Mean," "Matching Method to Message," and "General Guidelines" are adapted from Marion (2008b).

2. Indeed, using a white background is an unfortunate and outmoded artifact of overhead projectors, producing the greatest glare (and associated eye strain) possible. Using lighter colored fonts against dark backgrounds is one of the easiest, yet least used ways of providing strong visual impact.

REFERENCES

Alemu, Getaneh, Stevens, B., and Ross, P. (2011), "Semantic Metadata Interoperability in Digital Libraries: A Constructivist Grounded Theory Approach," ACM/IEEE Joint Conference on Digital Libraries, Ottawa, Canada, June 7–16.

Antonaki, Katerina (2008), "The-walk-in-the-city: a (no)ordinary image: an essay on creative technologies," in *Proceedings of the 3rd International Conference on Digital Interactive Media in Entertainment and Arts*. Athens, Greece: ACM.

Banks, Marcus, and Ruby, J. (2011), *Made to Be Seen: Perspectives on the History of Visual Anthropology*. Chicago: Chicago University Press.

Barbash, Ilisa, and Taylor, L. (1997), *Cross-Cultural Filmmaking: A Handbook for Making Documentary and Ethnographic Films and Videos*. Berkeley: University of California Press.

Barthes, Roland (1979/2010), *Camera Lucida: Reflections on Photography*. New York: Hill and Wang.

Bateson, Gregory, and Mead, M. (1942), *Balinese Character: A Photographic Analysis*. New York: New York Academy of Sciences.

Bateson, Gregory, and Mead, M. (1952), *Trance and Dance in Bali* (film, black-and-white, 22 minutes). Penn State Media.

Bateson, Gregory, and Mead, M. (1954a), *Bathing Babies in Three Cultures* (film, black-and-white, 11 minutes). Penn State Media.

Bateson, Gregory, and Mead, M. (1954b), *Childhood Rivalry in Bali and New Guinea* (film, black-and-white, 17 minutes). Penn State Media.

Becker, Howard S. (1986), "Do Photographs tell the Truth?" in *Doing Things Together: Selected Papers*. Evanston, IL: Northwestern University Press.

Benmayor, Rina (2008), "Digital Storytelling as a Signature Pedagogy for the New Humanities," *Arts and Humanities in Higher Education*, 7/2: 188–204.

Besteman, Catherine (2009), "The Somali Bantu Experience: Using Multimedia Ethnography for Community Building, Public Education and Advocacy," *Anthropology News*, 50/4: 23.

Bidwell, Nicola J., Reitmaier, T., Marsden, G., and Hansen, S. (2010), "Designing with Mobile Digital Storytelling in Rural Africa," in *Proceedings of the 28th International Conference on Human Factors in Computing Systems*. Atlanta, GA:ACM.

Biella, Peter (1996) "Interactive Media in Anthropology: Seed and Earth—Promise of Rain," *American Anthropologist*, 98/3: 595–616.

Biella, Peter (2001), "The Legacy of John Collier, Jr.," *Visual Anthropology Review*, 17/2: 50–60.

Biella, Peter (2009a), "Visual Anthropology in a Time of War: Intimacy and Interactivity in Ethnographic Media," in Mary Strong and Laena Wilder (eds.), *Viewpoints: Visual Anthropologists at Work*. Austin: University of Texas Press.

Biella, Peter (2009b), "Elementary Forms of the Digital Media," in Mary Strong and Laena Wilder (eds.), *Viewpoints: Visual Anthropologists at Work*. Austin: University of Texas Press.

Biella, Peter, Chagnon, N. A., and Seaman, G. (1997), *Yanomamö: The Ax Fight* (Case Studies in Cultural Anthropology multimedia series). Orlando, FL: Harcourt Brace & Co.

Bishop, John M., and Bishop, N. (1997/2002), *Himalayan Herders* (DVD, 76 minutes). Portland, OR: Media Generation.

Bishop, John M., and Leppzer, R. (1982), *Choose Life* (video, 10 minutes). Portland, OR: Media Generation.

Blue, Carroll P., and Kang, K. H. A. (2003), *The Dawn At My Back: Memoir of a Black Texas Upbringing—An Interactive Cultural History* (DVD). Los Angeles: Annenberg Center for Communications.

Boellstroff, Tom (2008), *Coming of Age in Second Life: An Anthropologist Explores the Virtually Human*. Princeton, NJ: Princeton University Press.

Bourdieu, Pierre (2012), *Picturing Algeria*. New York: Columbia University Press.

Brooks, David (2011), *Digital Darkroom Resource* (CD-ROM, Edition 4.3). Lompoc, CA: Author.

Brown, Pete (2011), "Us and Them: Who Benefits from Experimental Exhibition Making?" *Museum Management and Curatorship*, 26/2: 129–48.

Buckley, Liam (2001), "Self and Accessory in Gambian Studio Photography," *Visual Anthropology Review*, 16/2: 71–91.

Buckley, Liam (2005), "Objects of Love and Decay: Colonial Photographs in a Postcolonial Archive," *Cultural Anthropology*, 20/2: 249–70.

Bull, Stephen (2010), *Photography*. New York: Routledge.

Cartwright, Elizabeth, and Romero, M. (2009), "Lifeflight Ventilator Project: Identifying Teaching Styles in a Critical Care Setting Using Videotaped Data," presented at Annual Kasiska College of Health Professions Research Day, Pocatello, Idaho, February.

Chaplin, Elizabeth (1994), *Sociology and Visual Representations*. London: Routledge.

Chio, Jenny (2011), "Know Yourself: Making the Visual Work in Tourism Research," in C. Michael Hall (ed.), *Fieldwork in Tourism: Methods, Issues, Reflections*. New York: Routledge.

Collier, John Jr. (1997), "Cultural Energy Lecture, Field Museum of Natural History, Chicago September 19, 1987," *Visual Anthropology Review*, 13/2: 48–67.

Collier, John Jr., and Collier, M. (1967/1986), *Visual Anthropology: Photography as Research Method*. Albuquerque: University of New Mexico Press.

Crawford, Peter I., and Simonsen, J. K., eds. (1992), *Ethnographic Film Aesthetics and Narrative Tradition: Proceedings from NAFA2*. Aarhus, Denmark: Intervention Press.

Crehan, Kate (2011), *Community Art: An Anthropological Perspective*. London: Berg.

Crowder, Jerome (2003), "Living on the Edge: A Photographic Essay on Urban Aymara Migrants in El Alto, Bolivia," *Visual Anthropology*, 16/2: 263–87.

Crowder, Jerome (2006), "Visual Anthropology," in H. James Birx (ed.), *Encyclopedia of Anthropology*. Thousand Oaks, CA: Sage.

Crowder, Jerome (2007), "Aymara Migrants in El Alto, Bolivia: A Photographic Essay," in Ray Hutchinson and Jerome Krase (eds.), *Ethnic Landscapes in a Global World* (Research in Urban Sociology Series). New York: Elsevier Press.

Curtis, Edward (1914), *In the Land of the Head Hunters* (film, silent, black-and-white, 47 minutes). World Film Co.

Deacon, David (2007), *Researching Communications: A Practical Guide to Methods in Media and Cultural Analysis*. London: Hodder Arnold.

Debes, John L. (1969), "The Loom of Visual Literacy," *Audiovisual Instruction*, 14/8: 25–7.

Dowdall, George W., and Golden, J. (1989), "Photographs as Data: An Analysis of Images from a Mental Hospital," *Qualitative Sociology*, 12/2: 183–213.

Durington, Matthew, and Ruby, J. (2011), "Ethnographic Film," in Marcus Banks and Jay Ruby (eds.), *Made to Be Seen: Perspectives on the History of Visual Anthropology*. Chicago: University of Chicago Press.

Edwards, Elizabeth, ed. (1994), *Anthropology and Photography: 1860–1920*. New Haven, CT: Yale University Press.

Edwards, Elizabeth (2011), "Tracing Photography," in Marcus Banks and Jay Ruby (eds.), *Made to Be Seen: Perspectives on the History of Visual Anthropology*.Chicago: University of Chicago Press.

El Guindi, Fadwa (2004), *Visual Anthropology: Essential Method and Theory*. Walnut Creek, CA: AltaMira Press.

Engelbrecht, Beate, ed. (2007), *Memories of the Origins of Ethnographic Film*. New York: Peter Lang.

Erlmann, Veit, ed. (2004), *Hearing Cultures: Essays on Sound, Listening and Modernity*. Oxford: Berg.

Ericksen, Julia (2011), *Dance With Me: Ballroom Dancing and the Promise of Instant Intimacy*. New York: New York University Press.

Feld, Steven (1990), *Sound and Sentiment: Birds, Weeping, Poetics and Song in Kaluli Expression*, 2nd ed. Philadelphia: University of Pennsylvania Press.

Feld, Steven, and Brenneis, D. (2004), "Doing Anthropology in Sound," *American Ethnologist*, 31/4: 461–44.

Flaherty, Robert (1922), *Nanook of the North* (film, silent, black-and-white, 79 minutes). The Criterion Collection.

Freeman, Michael (2007), *The Photographer's Eye: Composition and Design for Better Digital Photos*. Boston: Focal Press.

Freeman, Richard (2009), "Photography and Ethnography," in Mary Strong and Laena Wilder (eds.), *Viewpoints: Visual Anthropologists at Work*. Austin: University of Texas Press.

Gardner, Robert (1963), *Dead Birds* (film, 83 minutes). Documentary Education Resources.

Goldstein, Barry M. (2007), "All Photos Lie: Images as Data," in Gregory C. Stanczak (ed.), *Visual Research Methods: Image, Society and Representation*. Thousand Oaks, CA: Sage.

Greenberg, Jane (2009), "Metadata and Digital Information," in *Encyclopedia of Library and Information Sciences*, 3rd ed. Boca Raton, FL: CRC Press.

Grimshaw, Anna, and Ravetz, A., eds. (2005), *Visualizing Anthropology*. Bristol: Intellect Books.

Grimshaw, Anna, and Ravetz, A. (2009), *Observational Cinema: Anthropology, Film, and the Exploration of Social Life*. Bloomington: Indian University Press.

Gubrium, Aline (2009), "Digital Storytelling as a Method for Engaged Scholarship in Anthropology," *Practicing Anthropology*, 31/4: 5–9.

Guillemin, Marilys, and Drew, S. (2010), "Questions of Process in Participant-Generated Visual Methodologies," *Visual Studies*, 25/2: 175–88.

Harper, Douglas (1988), "Visual Sociology: Expanding Sociological Vision," *The American Sociologist*, Spring: 54–70.

Harper, Douglas (2002), Talking About Pictures: A Case for Photo Elicitation," *Visual Studies*, 17/1: 13–26.

Harper, Douglas (2003), "Reimagining Visual Methods: Galileo to Neuromancer," in Norman Denzin and Yvonne Lincoln (eds.), *Collecting and Interpreting Qualitative Materials*. Thousand Oaks, CA: Sage.

Hastrup, Kirsten (1992), "Anthropological Visions: Some Notes on Visual and Textual Authority," in Peter I. Crawford and David Turton (eds.), *Film as Ethnography*. Manchester: Manchester University Press.

Heider, Karl (2006), *Ethnographic Film*. Austin: University of Texas Press.

Heider, Karl, Blakely, P., and Blakely, T. (2007), *Seeing Anthropology: Cultural Anthropology through Film*, 4th ed. Boston: Allyn & Bacon.

Henley, Paul (2007), "Seeing, Hearing, Feeling: Sound and the Despotism of the Eye in 'Visual' Anthropology," *Visual Anthropology Review*, 23/1: 54–63.

Hine, Christine (2000) *Virtual Ethnography*. Thousand Oaks, CA: Sage.

Hine, Christine, ed. (2005), *Virtual Methods*. Oxford: Berg.

Hockings, Paul, ed. (1975/2003), *Principles of Visual Anthropology*. The Hague: Mouton.

Hopkins, Candice (2006), "Making Things Our Own: The Indigenous Aesthetic in Digital Storytelling," *Leonardo*, 39/4: 341–44.

Idris, Fayez, and Panchanathan, S. (1997), "Review of Image and Video Indexing Techniques," *Journal of Visual Communication and Image Representation*, 8/2: 146–66.

Iverson, Gunnar, and Simonsen, J. K., eds. (2010), *Beyond the Visual: Sound and Image in Ethnographic and Documentary Film*. Aarhus, Denmark: Intervention Press.

Jacknis, Ira (1984), "Franz Boas and Photography," *Studies in Visual Communication*, 10/1: 2–60.

Jay, Martin (1994), *Downcast Eyes: The Denigration of Vision in Twentieth-Century French Thought*. Berkeley: University of California Press.

Jenks, Chris (1995), "The Centrality of the Eye in Western Culture: An Introduction," in Chris Jenks (ed.), *Visual Culture*. London: Routledge.

Kera, Denisa, and Graham, C. (2010), "Living Avatars Network: Fusing Traditional and Innovative Ethnographic Methods through a Real-time Mobile Video Service," *Ethnographic Praxis in Industry Conference Proceedings*, 2010/1: 149–68.

Kottak, Conrad P. (2011), "Melvin Ember and HRAF, Anthropology's Archive," *Cross-Cultural Research*, 45/1: 11–15.

Kozinets, Robert V. (2009), *Netnography: Doing Ethnographic Research Online*. Thousand Oaks, CA: Sage.

Lajoux, Jean-Dominique (1975/2003), "Ethnographic Film and History," in Paul Hockings (ed.), *Principles of Visual Anthropology*. The Hague: Mouton.

Lambert, Joseph (2009), *Digital Storytelling: Capturing Lives, Creating Community*, 2nd ed. Berkeley, CA: Digital Diner Press.

Lange, Holley R. (2009), "Metadata," *Technical Services Quarterly*, 27/1: 139–41.

Lave, Jean, and Wenger, E. (1991), *Situated Learning: Legitimate Peripheral Participation*. Cambridge: Cambridge University Press.

Levy, Thomas E., Anderson, J.D., Waggoner, M., Smith, N., Muniz, A., and Adams, R. B. (2001), "Interface: Archaeology and Technology—Digital Archaeology 2001: GIS-Based Excavation Recording in Jordan," *The SAA Archaeological Record*, 1: 23–9.

Levy, Thomas E., and Smith, N. G. (2007), "On-Site Digital Archaeology: GIS-Based Excavation Recording in Southern Jordan," in T. E. Levy, M. Daviau, R. Younker, and M. M. Shaer (eds.), *Crossing Jordan–North American Contributions to the Archaeology of Jordan*. London: Equinox.

Levy, Thomas E., Petrovic, V., Wypych, T., Gidding, A., Knabb, K., et al. (2010), "On-Site Digital Archaeology 3.0 and Cyber-Archaeology: Into the Future of the Past—New Developments, Delivery and the Creation of a Data Avalanche," in Maurizio Forte (ed.), *Cyber-Archaeology*. Oxford: Archaeopress.

Lutz, Catherine, and Collins, J. (1991), "The Photograph as an Intersection of Gazes: The Example of National Geographic," *Visual Anthropology Review*, 7/1: 134–49.

Lutz, Catherine, and Collins, J. (1993), *Reading National Geographic*. Chicago: University of Chicago Press.

MacDougal, David (1975/2003), "Beyond Observational Cinema," in Paul Hockings (ed.), *Principles of Visual Anthropology*. The Hague: Mouton.

MacDougal, David (1997–98/2000), *Doon School Chronicles* (DVD, 140 minutes). Berkeley, CA: Berkeley Media LLC.

MacDougal, David (2006), *The Corporeal Image: Film, Ethnography, and the Senses*. Princeton: Princeton University Press.

MacDougal, David, and MacDougal, J. (1974), *To Live with Herds* (DVD, black-and-white, 70 minutes). Berkeley, CA: Berkeley Media LLC.

Marion, Jonathan S. (2008a), *Ballroom: Culture and Costume in Competitive Dance*. Oxford: Berg.

Marion, Jonathan S. (2008b), "Using Visuals in Conference Papers and Panels: Showing What You Mean," *Anthropology News*, 49/3: 62.

Marion, Jonathan S. (2010), "Photography as Ethnographic Passport," *Visual Anthropology Review*, 26/1: 24–30.

Marion, Jonathan S. (2011), "Introduction to Photographing an Emotion," in Julia Ericksen (ed.), *Dance With Me: Ballroom Dancing and the Promise of Instant Intimacy*. New York: New York University Press.

Marion, Jonathan S. (2012), "Circulation as Destination: Considerations from the Translocal Culture of Competitive Ballroom Dance," *Journal for the Anthropological Study of Human Movement*, 17/2. <http://jashm.press.illinois.edu/17.2/index.html> accessed September 12, 2012.

McClean, Shilo T. (2007), *Digital Storytelling: The Narrative Power of Visual Effects in Film*. Cambridge, MA: MIT Press.

Mead, Margaret (1975/2003), "Introduction," in Paul Hockings (ed.), *Principles of Visual Anthropology*. New York: Mouton de Gruyter.

Miller, Daniel, and Slater, D. (2001), *The Internet: An Ethnographic Approach*. Oxford: Berg.

Milne, Elisabeth-Jane, Mitchell, C. A., and de Lange, N., eds. (2012), *Handbook of Participatory Video*. Lanham, MD: AltaMira Press.

Mitchell, Claudine (2011), *Doing Visual Research*. Los Angeles: Sage.

Morris, Errol (2011), *Believing Is Seeing: Observations on the Mysteries of Photography*. London: Penguin Press.

Nakamura, Karen (2010), *Bethel: Community and Schizophrenia in Northern Japan* (film, 41 minutes). Manic Productions.

Neal, Diane (2008), "News Photographers, Librarians, Tags, and Controlled Vocabularies: Balancing the Forces," *Journal of Library Metadata*, 8/3: 199–219.

Nichols, Bill (2010), *Introduction to Documentary*. Bloomington: Indiana University Press.

Nickel, Douglas R. (2001), "History of Photography: The State of Research," *The Art Bulletin*, 83/3: 548–558.

Nijland, Dirk J. (2006), "Ritual Performance and Visual Representations," in Metje Postma and Peter I. Crawford (eds.), *Reflecting Visual Ethnography: Using the Camera in Anthropological Research*. Leiden: CNWS Publications.

Papademas, Diana, and the International Visual Sociology Association (2009), "IVSA Code of Research Ethics and Guidelines," *Visual Studies*, 24/3: 250–7.

Peres, Michael R. (2007), *The Focal Encyclopedia of Photography: Digital Imaging, Theory and Applications, History and Science*. Boston: Focal Press.

Perry, Sara E. (2006), "Picturing Prehistory Within (and Without) Science: De-Constructing Archaeological Portrayals of the Peopling of New Territories." Unpublished MA thesis, University of Victoria, Victoria, Canada.

Perry, Sara E. (2009), "Fractured Media: Challenging the Dimensions of Archaeology's Typical Visual Modes of Engagement," *Archaeologies*, 5/3: 389–415.

Perry, Sara E. (2011), "The Archaeological Eye: Visualisation and the Institutionalisation of Academic Archaeology in London." Unpublished PhD dissertation, University of Southampton, Southampton, United Kingdom.

Perry, Sara and Marion, J. S. (2010), "State of the Ethics in Visual Anthropology?" *Visual Anthropology Review*, 26/2: 96–104.

Petrovic, V., Gidding, A., Wypych, T., Kuester, F., DeFanti, T. A., and Levy, T. E. (2011), "Dealing with Archaeology's Data Avalanche," *Computer*, July: 56–60.

Pink, Sarah (2006), *The Future of Visual Anthropology: Engaging the Senses*. New York: Routledge.

Pink, Sarah (2009), *Doing Visual Ethnography*, 2nd ed. Thousand Oaks, CA: Sage.

Pink, Sarah (2011), "Doing Visual Anthropology: Potentials and Challenges," in Marcus Banks and Jay Ruby (eds.), *Made to Be Seen: Perspectives on the History of Visual Anthropology*. Chicago: University of Chicago Press.

Pink, Sarah, Kürti, L., and Afonso, A. I. (2004), *Working Images: Visual Research and Representation in Ethnography*. New York: Routledge.

Pinney, Christopher (2011), *Photography and Anthropology*. London: Reaktion Books.

Postma, Metje, and Crawford, P. I. (2006), "Introduction. Visual Ethnography and Anthropology," in Metje Postma and Peter I. Crawford (eds.), *Reflecting Visual Ethnography: Using the Camera in Anthropological Research*. Leiden: CNWS Publications.

Reilly, Karen, and Nancy Singleton, N. (2008), "Cataloging Images in Millennium: A Central Repository for Faculty-Owned Images," *Journal of Library Metadata*, 8/1: 37–42.

Riis, Jacob A. (1890/1997), *How the Other Half Lives: Studies Among the Tenements of New York*. New York: Penguin Classics.

Roberts, Allen F. (2000), "Review of *African Ceremonies* by Carol Beckwith and Angela Fisher," *African Arts*, 33/3: 10–2, 93–4.

Robin, Bernard R. (2008), "Digital Storytelling: A Powerful Technology Tool for the 21st Century Classroom," *Theory Into Practice*, 47/3: 220–8

Rodden, Kerry, and Wood, K. R. (2003), "How do people manage their digital photographs?" in *Proceedings of the SIGCHI conference on Human factors in Computing Systems*. Fort Lauderdale, FL: ACM.

Rose, Gillian (2007), *Visual Methodologies: An Introduction to the Interpretation of Visual Materials*, 2nd ed. Thousand Oaks, CA: Sage.

Rouch, Jean, and Feld, S. (2003), *Ciné-ethnography*. Minneapolis: University of Minnesota Press.

Ruby, Jay (2000), *Picturing Culture*. Chicago: University of Chicago Press.

Russotti, Patricia, and Anderson, R. (2009), *Digital Photography Best Practices and Workflow Handbook: A Guide to Staying Ahead of the Workflow Curve*. Boston: Focal Press.

Scherer, Joanna C. (1975/2003), "Ethnographic Photography in Anthropological Research," in Paul Hockings (ed.), *Principles of Visual Anthropology*. The Hague: Mouton.

Scherer, Joanna C. (1990), "Historical Photographs as Anthropological Documents: A Retrospect," *Visual Anthropology*, 3/2–3: 131–55.

Scherer, Joanna C., and DeMallie, R. J., eds. (2013), *Life Among the Indians*. Lincoln: University of Nebraska Press.

Schneider, Arnd, and Wright, C., eds. (2006), *Between Art and Anthropology: Contemporary Ethnographic Practice*. Oxford: Berg.

Schneider, Arnd, and Wright, C., eds. (2006), *Contemporary Art and Anthropology*. Oxford: Berg.

Simoni, Simonetta (1996), "The Visual Essay: Redefining Data, Presentation and Scientific Truth," *Visual Sociology*, 11/2: 75–82.

Smith, Tim (2010), "In Poor Light," *Interventions*, 12/2: 198–208.

Sontag, Susan (1973/2001), *On Photography*. New York: Picador.

Sontag, Susan (2003), *Regarding the Pain of Others*. New York: Picador.

Spencer, Stephen (2011), *Visual Research Methods in the Social Sciences: Awakening Visions*. New York: Routledge.

Sroka, Marek (2011), "Identifying and Interpreting Prewar and Wartime Jewish Photographs in Polish Digital Collections," *Slavic & East European Information Resources*, 12/2–3: 175–87.

Steinmueller, Uwe, and Gulbins, J. (2010), *The Digital Photography Workflow Handbook: From Import to Output*. Sebastopol, CA: Rocky Nook.

Sterritt, David (2000), "Revision, Prevision, and the Aura of Improvisatory Art," *The Journal of Aesthetics and Art Criticism*, 58/2: 163–72.

Strand, Paul (1917), "Photography," *Camera Work*, 49/50: 3.

Strong, Mary, and Wilder, L., eds. (2009), *Viewpoints: Visual Anthropologists at Work*. Austin: University of Texas Press.

Svasek, Maruska (2007), *Anthropology, Art and Cultural Production: Histories, Themes, Perspectives*. London: Pluto Press.

Thom, Randy (2003), "Designing a Movie for Sound," in Larry Sider, Dianne Freeman, and Jerry Sider (eds.), *Soundscape: The School of Sound Lectures 1998–2001*. New York: Wallflower Press.

Tomaselli, Keyan G. (1996), *Appropriating Images: The Semiotics of Visual Representation*. Højbjerg, Denmark: Intervention Press.

Tufte, Edward R. (2006), *Beautiful Evidence*. Cheshire, CT: Graphics Press.

Viditz-Ward, Vera (2000), "Review of *African Ceremonies* by Carol Beckwith & Angela Fisher," *African Arts*, 33/3: 9–10.

Wesch, Michael (2007), *The Machine is Us/ing Us*. <http://www.youtube.com/watch?v=NLlGopyXT_g> accessed May 12, 2012.

Westermann, Mariet, ed. (2005), *Anthropologies of Art*. Williamstown, MA: Clark Art Institute.

Wheeler, R.E. Mortimer (1927), "History by Excavation," *Journal of the Royal Society of Arts*, 75: 814–34.

Wolowic, Jennifer (2007), *For Our Street Family* (DVD, 34 minutes). Watertown, MA: Documentary Educational Resources.

Wright, Terence (2004), *The Photography Handbook*, 2nd ed. London: Routledge.

Wright, Terence (2009), *Visual Impact: Culture and the Meaning of Images*. Oxford: Berg.

Wulff, Helena (2007), "Longing for the Land: Emotions, Memory, and Nature in Irish Travel Advertisements," *Identities: Global Studies in Culture and Power*, 14: 527–44.

Young, Colin (1975/2003), "Observational Cinema," in Paul Hockings (ed.), *Principles of Visual Anthropology*. The Hague: Mouton.

Young, Michael, and Clark, J. (2002), *An Anthropologist in Papua: The Photography of F.E. Williams, 1922–39*. London: C. Hurst & Company.

Zakia, Richard D., and Page, D. A. (2011), *Photographic Composition: A Visual Guide*. Boston: Focal Press.

Zavoina, Susan, and Reichert, T. (2000), "Media Convergence/Management Change: The Evolving Workflow for Visual Journalists," *Journal of Media Economics*, 13/2: 143–51.

INDEX

Page numbers in *italics* refer to figures
Page numbers in **bold** refer to case studies
Information in notes is indexed in the form 149n5.1, which indicates page 149, chapter 5, note 1

composition, 70–1
  evaluating, 77–8
  intent, 68–9
  lighting, 73–6
  nonverbal signals, 73, *75*
  pitfalls, 70–7
  practice, 76–7, *77*
  resources, 80
  stability, 70, *71*, 150n6.4
  training use, **69**
  zoom, 150n6.5
Vimeo, 72, 89
viruses, 153n10.4
visual ethics, 5–11
  see also ethics
visual literacy, 13

webpages, 88–9, 150n7.5
  see also Internet
white balance, 75–6, 149n5.6
wide angle lens, 60–1
wildcards, 118–19
Williams, F. E., 42, *43*, 46
Wolowic, Jennifer, **78–9,** *79*
workflow, 98, *99*
Wright, Terence, **63–5,** *64*

Yanomamo Interactive, 87
YouTube, 72, 89

Zeki, Semir, 31
Zeller, Anne, **34–6**
zoom lens, 59, 149n5.2, 150n6.5